THE RAMPARTS WE WATCH

BY

LUTHER W. YOUNGDAHL

*Judge of the United States District Court
for the District of Columbia, and former
Governor of the State of Minnesota.*

Publishers

T. S. DENISON & COMPANY, INC.

Minneapolis

Printed in the U. S. A.
By THE BRINGS PRESS

Dedication

I dedicate this volume to my loyal, devoted wife, Irene. Throughout our thirty-eight years of marital companionship she has been a continual inspiration to me. She is a living example of one who not only professes her faith in God and love for her fellow men, but practices this faith in all the relationships of life.

Contents

Preface

I write this preface on the day following the announcement by the Soviet Union that it intends to resume testing nuclear bombs. Ominous as the crisis produced by this decision may be, I am confident that our Government will have successfully met the challenge and countered the threat by the time this book appears.

However, I am not so certain that we as American citizens shall have responded sufficiently to the long-term overriding demand which each generation of Americans faces: that we fulfill, at home and abroad, the injunction of our Constitution to "secure the blessings of liberty to ourselves and our posterity."

How we fulfill this pledge—how, in short, we maintain the ramparts we watch—is of great importance, of course, to each of our own citizens. But today, with the world watching the ramparts with us, our response is vital to our image in the eyes of people everywhere.

Thus far I am convinced, after trips around the world—most recently to South America—that the world is not impressed by what it has seen. This is true chiefly because we have not indicated with sufficient clarity and conviction which of our institutions we really consider our bulwarks, our ramparts. Are they our factories or our families? Our tailfins or our faith in God? Our military stockpile or our schools? In short, our hardware or our hopes for individual dignity and equality before God and man?

In the chapters which follow, I have attempted to give my answers to these questions and my concept of the ramparts we and the world must watch and preserve for freedom's survival. In essence, I have stated my belief that the greatness of this country and the ultimate road to the greatest good for all mankind is not manufacturing output or military strength—necessary though they may be—nor a political system; rather, the key to a great society is that which opens its heart and releases reverence for human life and respect for individual dignity. And the engine of such a society is a citizenry which recognizes these principles and participates in the planning and execution of programs to strengthen the ramparts they embody.

In the last three chapters of the book I have presented excerpts from the Inaugural messages given to the Minnesota legislature during my three terms as Governor in 1947, 1949 and 1951. In these messages I urged the adoption of programs which if enacted and properly administered would, I believe, strengthen our important ramparts, promote honesty and humanity in government, preserve the dignity of every individual and reverence for human life.

—LUTHER W. YOUNGDAHL

CHAPTER I

The Tyranny of Words

I should like to discuss with you a disease with which I believe the people of the nation are afflicted—the disease of the tyranny of words. By this I mean that we have in too many areas of our national life pledged loyalty to the great concepts of our society, failing to realize that reiteration of the phrases without applying their teachings to practical problems renders them mere shibboleths.

What we have forgotten is that those who composed our statements of national dedication—the Declaration of Independence with its ringing proclamation that all men are created equal and endowed with the inalienable right to life, liberty, and the pursuit of happiness; the pledge of allegiance to the Flag: one nation under God, with liberty and justice for all—did not infuse these lamplights of freedom with an eternal flame. What they did was to start us on the right path with the opportunity to rekindle the flame as the circumstances of each generation required.

Instead, what we have allowed ourselves to believe is that our statements of purpose are self-executing—that proclaiming ourselves a nation under God has made us so for all time;

11

that verbal devotion to "equal justice under law" without more, is enough. What many of us also fail to realize is that participation in the process of turning these words into deeds is an exciting experience and that each of us, no matter what his position, must participate in this process if the pledges are to be fulfilled and if freedom is to be maintained.

Let us look at a few examples of this gap between pledge and performance.

I

Our basic proclamation to each other and to the world is that all men are endowed with the "inalienable right" to "life, liberty, and the pursuit of happiness." Basic to effectuation of this pledge is a proper start in life for our young people. Are they being afforded this start?

First, are they receiving strong and warm home guidance, discipline, inspiration and spiritual training?

When we say we believe in a nation of strong families, have these words become mere shibboleths?

The importance of the family is reflected in the Chinese proverb, "As goes the home, so goes the nation; as goes the nation, so goes the world."

It is now axiomatic in American life that the family is a sacred institution. This most sacred human relationship, ordained by God Himself, is a vital part of Judaeo-Christian tradition. It is in the home that the lessons of mutual responsibility and of self-sacrifice are learned.

Every child is entitled to a normal home and to the friendship, recognition, wholesome adventure, discipline and spiritual guidance which parents should provide. In the home each individual must be accorded the opportunity to achieve physical, mental and spiritual maturity. And yet the record discloses a serious decline in the integrity of the home. We have been confronted with a steadily growing list of statistics about the weakening of the family; the divorce rate continues high; divorces mean broken homes; and broken homes mean children who are innocent victims. Out of these broken homes comes a tragic amount of youth delinquency and the loss of precious human resources.

There is an ominous similarity to the disintegration of the family when Rome declined and the condition of far too many families in Western civilization today. When the disintegration of the Roman family system had been finally consummated and diffused throughout the Roman Empire, it only epitomized the general dissolution of the social structure as a whole and became the vehicle of the collapse of that structure of civilization.

Second, are our young people receiving the educational opportunities essential to full development of their potential as individuals—and incidentally, to our strength as a nation? When we have repeatedly emphasized the importance of equality of educational opportunity have these, likewise, been empty words?

Education is of critical importance in a democracy. Thomas Jefferson spoke for America when he said, "By far the most important bill in our whole code is that for the diffusion of knowledge among the people. No other sure foundation can be devised for the preservation of freedom and happiness." The American way of life demands that every citizen shall have the right to an education. Its enemies thrive on ignorance and illiteracy. The American ideal of educational equality is far short of attainment, as draft rejections during both world wars amply proved. We have a long way to go and critical times such as these ought to spur us on to a new zeal to provide an education to meet the demands of the hour.

It is interesting to recall that the act establishing our land grant colleges, after years of controversy in Congress and a Presidential veto, was finally signed by Lincoln a century ago. It is the development of these colleges which has made America the foremost agricultural and industrial nation in the world. Our own State University, as one of the land grant colleges, has grown to be one of the greatest institutions of higher education in the nation. It has become great because the people of Minnesota early recognized its worth and have been willing to pay for its continued growth. To meet the needs of this space age it will require even greater support.

We face a new situation in education for two reasons: During the early 1940's about two million babies were born each year in the United States. During the latter 1940's, the number increased to more than four million and has continued at that figure since. This means that as this larger group moves up through the grades and into high school and college there must be twice as many classrooms and twice as many teachers merely to maintain the quantity demand for education.

But there is also a quality demand. We cannot hold our place in the race for world supremacy without greatly improving the quality of our education. We are more conscious just now of the need for improved education in science and technology to meet the Russian threat. However, the need is equally great for historians and philosophers and leaders in the humanities. We cannot afford to allow our education to be thrown out of balance by our efforts to match our rivals.

Third, when home and school fail in giving a youngster the proper start in life and he drifts into juvenile delinquency, is the pledge to give *all* men the right to life, liberty, and the pursuit of happiness fulfilled? Again, I am afraid that it is not—that Shakespeare's warning in "Hamlet" about the superficiality of words, words, words might well apply to our actions in this area.

In dealing with the individual offender, we still employ too frequently the quick, simple, retributive solution of punishment. Crimes of violence are, of course, a cause for profound concern. But there are elements of real hysteria in some of the current reactions to them, effectively illustrated, I believe, in a recent cartoon in the "Manchester Guardian" which portrayed five citizens carrying banners with the inscriptions: "Flog 'em," "Reasoning Doesn't Help," "Hang 'em," "Birch 'em," "Join our Anti-Violence League."

But more important, we fail to understand that the only effective way to massively reduce the incidence of crime is to exterminate its roots—the roots of slums, overcrowded schools, denial of job opportunities because of race and color of skin, neglect of children who through no fault of their own are born to parents who give them neither discipline, love, care, nor religious guidance, nor even sustenance. Those who thus begin life as second-class citizens are entitled to society's care, not its condemnation.

II.

We profess our reverence for life and the dignity of the individual. Have we carried this profession into practice in respect to our mentally ill?

What is the magnitude of the problem of mental illness? It is seventeen million of our citizens suffering from some form of mental illness—one in every ten persons.

It is ten per cent of public school children emotionally disturbed and in need of mental guidance.

It is at least two hundred thousand other children receiving treatment each year at mental health clinics throughout the country.

It is approximately five million, four hundred thousand children and adults mentally retarded—about three per cent of our entire population.

The extent of mental disease and retardation, in short, is great. Its role as a factor in criminal behavior, delinquency, suicide, alcoholism, and narcotic addiction is, sadly, a significant one.

Our past performance in dealing with the problem has been a poor one.

To assist disturbed school children, the majority of our schools lack trained personnel or facilities.

To care for those needing hospitalization, our State mental institutions are generally inadequate—a large percentage of them being overcrowded and many failing to meet the minimum standards established by the American Psychiatric Association.

To care for those patients fortunate enough to secure hospital admission, funds are shockingly meager—in 1959 the average amount spent for research per individual hospital case, employing federal, state, national volunteer health agency and other private funds was approximately $96.

To care for those needing clinical treatment, there are only 1400 clinics in the entire country—almost all with waiting lists of from three months to a year. There should be at least 3600 such clinics—more than twice as many as we have.

Finally, in response to the long and tragic history of our care of the mentally ill in this country, we have seen vast periods of public apathy punctuated by sporadic outbursts of citizen indignation leading to patchwork and only partial reforms in many of our state hospitals.

Our needs in this field should be painfully obvious. First, more funds for research to discover cures and better methods of prevention, care and treatment. Second, training of additional psychiatrists, psychiatric social workers and nurses to give more efficient care to the increasing number of mentally ill. Third, larger and more ambitious programs for training the practitioner of psychiatric skills. Fourth, increased experimentation in the field of community mental health services. Fifth, development of out-patient services.

If a free society cannot help those who have fallen by the wayside, then what good are all its six-lane turnpikes and its elaborate mechanical gadgets? Though we have made substantial progress in the last two decades in the care of the mentally ill, thousands still remain the lostlings of society, made mute by sickness, guarded walls and the loss of their civil rights. Casualties of the spirit, voiceless and powerless, their very personalities—yes, their very lives—are completely dependent on the concern, wisdom and compassion of those who are more fortunate. Nowhere is man's inhumanity to man more pronounced than in the care of the mentally ill.

And how do we apply our professed belief in reverence for life as to our senior citizens? The White House Conference on Aging, held at the Nation's Capital in January, 1961, produced some significant facts, among some of which were as follows:

The average man or woman can expect to live longer than ever before—into his 70's and 80's. More people will have longer periods of retirement. At age 60 in 1900, for example, a man could expect less than three years in retirement. Today he can expect more than eight retirement years.

We have sixteen million people over sixty-five today. This is five times more than we had in 1900 and the number will double in the next forty years. The number over 75 will triple. To these senior citizens we owe a responsibility. As stated in the Senior Citizens' Charter, "Each of our senior citizens, regardless of race, color or creed, is entitled to the right to be useful, the right to continue in at least part time employment, to be free from want in old age, the right to a fair share of the community's recreational, educational and medical resources, the right to obtain decent housing, the right to live and die in dignity." Of course, with these rights as stated in the Charter go certain obligations—among which are the following: "The obligation of each citizen to prepare himself to become active, alert, capable, self-supporting and useful; the obligation to learn and apply sound principles of physical and mental health; the obligation to seek and develop potential avenues of service in the years after retirement and the obligation to attempt to maintain such relations with family, neighbors and friends as will make him a respected and valued counsellor throughout his later years."

III.

Our basic national premise—the heart of the Judaeo-

Christian heritage to which we are heirs—is respect for the equal dignity of all individuals. Proudly we have chiseled into the marble facade of our Supreme Court: "Equal Justice Under Law," and yet when we repeat the pledge "With Justice for all," do we mean it? Are these, too, but idle words?

One of the most potent weapons in the arsenal of communism is the allegation that we as a people give no more than lip service to the Bill of Rights; that we loudly proclaim allegiance to equality, but actually practice racial and religious discrimination in our daily lives.

The struggle with communism is essentially a spiritual battle. Diplomatic maneuvers and supremacy in arms will never be sufficient to win the hearts of a billion people who, shaking off the shackles of the centuries, are demanding equality as dignified human beings.

In this day of nuclear energy and rocket projectiles, the whole human race is involved in a struggle for survival. Each one of us is a part of that struggle; the gist of the problem is the individual. It is the problem of being able to live with one another in the basic relationships of life—as husband and wife, parents and children, employer and employee, white men and Negroes, Protestants, Catholics and Jews. Every unfair discrimination a white man practices against a Negro in our community relationships, every nasty slur voiced by a Gentile against a Jew, every act of discourtesy or prejudice makes less possible the solution of mankind's gigantic problem.

The uncommitted nations of the world will be convinced by our actions and not by our words. Mrs. Youngdahl and I were at a private dinner party with Prime Minister Nehru in Delhi, India, at the time of the Little Rock incident. We saw at first hand the deterioration of respect for us as a democratic nation because of this tragic spectacle. What happened at Little Rock and what has happened more recently in Louisiana, Alabama and Mississippi has made front page news in a great many countries of the world. The harm done to the standing of the United States by such social violence is incalculable. The issue goes far beyond the states of the South involved in these unfortunate incidents.

The United States is beset with an all-encompassing cold war and is engaged in a battle for men's minds. A world two-thirds non-white looks critically at American pretensions. The growing question today is whether there is yet time for us to secure the respect of other people by our deeds rather than by our words.

Our solemn duty is to build bridges of understanding across the tragic chasms of racial, religious and national differences. Unless the social tensions are mitigated—and that right soon—they threaten to wrench the fabric of our society and tear it into shreds. Here, then, is a task which our heritage should inspire us to accomplish, and our role as a competitor for the hearts of the skeptical, uncommitted people of the world demands that we accomplish. To be true to our past and to secure our future, it is a task in which we must not fail.

IV.

Finally, we pledge that we are a nation under God, but have not these words also become mere shibboleths? Is it not true, as someone has said, that "Words eat men"?

In recent years we have come to realize that we are engaged in real competition with the Soviets in the economic, political and military fields and we cannot be too sure of victory in these areas. There is one issue, however, in which we can be sure to win—in maintaining the dignity of the individual and the moral and spiritual integrity of our people.

The real difference between the Soviet system and our system is that we profess we are and strive to live as a nation under God, and yet there are ominous signs that we are straying from the path. The great issue facing Americans in this space age is how to get off the launching pad of moral and spiritual deterioration, how to be strong so we can continue to be free—strong not only economically, politically and militarily, but more especially morally and spiritually. It is in this area that we have the real opportunity for victory.

Character always has and always will be the keystone of greatness in a person and in a whole nation. The historian can quickly show us that just as soon as the character of a people begins to weaken and break down, a nation begins to crumble and is on the road downward to ruin.

It seems to me we have somehow failed to impress the peoples in other areas of the world as to the vital theory which we believe makes our country great—its spiritual quality—and our belief in the worth of every individual.

Integrity of the people rather than material strength is what builds a nation. When French philosopher De Tocqueville visited America many years ago, he said, "America is great because America is good and if America ever ceases to be good, America will cease to be great."

A few examples will suffice to indicate a decline in our national character:

In the field of fraud, in 1958, bad checks that came to the notice of the F.B.I. had a face value of eight million dollars.

Daily press releases of the Federal Trade Commission reveal misrepresentation by sellers of goods as to origin, quality and price.

Householders have found themselves the victims of slipshod work and padded bills for repairs to the home or the family car.

Unscrupulous persons on relief have fraudulently requested and received more money than the law permits.

Surety companies reveal that employee dishonesty can be safely estimated at somewhere between five hundred million and one billion dollars a year.

Collusive arrangements between business and labor and television scandals have been revealed in recent Congressional investigations.

Corruption of law enforcement officers and other public officials and influence peddling have been disclosed in many quarters. Many more examples could be cited, but these instances should be sufficient to prove the necessity for strengthening the moral fibre of our society.

The beep, beep, beep of the satellite has been a familiar sound to one listening in an astronomic observatory in recent months. If one listened intently, it almost seemed the little satellite was saying to the people on earth, "Your time is short. You may have discovered a way to get to outer space, but unless you discover a way to peace, the conquest of space may well forecast the death of the world. It is the earth to which you should give importance. It has greater significance than the moon." The real issue is not whether one will get to the moon to beat any other nation, but will we get to the earth to save man from destruction?

Our problem has not changed with the coming of the space age. Though man should be successful in launching a bridgehead on the moon, or in finding possible living conditions on other planets, or perhaps in projecting a rocket into space with space pioneers ready to establish families and communities far beyond our earth in another solar system, our problem remains essentially the same—these courageous pioneers would have the same characteristics of human nature as those of the people they left behind. Our problem would still be man, himself. Therefore, though we must be willing to recognize our weaknesses, there are great days ahead if we will meet our challenges with discipline and dedication.

I like Carl Sandburg's vision of America's days ahead:

"I see America, not in the setting sun of a black night of despair ahead of us. I see America in the crimson light of a rising sun, fresh from the burning, creative hand of God. I see great days ahead— great days possible to men and women of will and vision."

Many years ago a great ship sank amid the icebergs of the Atlantic. A woman passenger waiting for a lifeboat received permission to return to her room where she kept her diamonds and other valuables. In this moment of danger, she ignored her jewels and instead snatched three oranges and made her way back to the lifeboat. In a lifeboat oranges take priority over diamonds. At the pivot between doom or dawn, human values become more precious than material values. In times of disaster, we see with a new vividness that material things will not insure our survival.

In today's hour of peril there must be a strong reaffirmation of the utter necessity for discipline, consecration and service.

It will be for all of us in the years ahead to determine whether oranges will be worth more than diamonds.

Chapter II

The Lostlings of Society

Mental health is the responsibility of state governments
—but it is also everybody's business.

Mental illness is not confined to the poor or lowly. It
strikes at all levels of our social order. The plea of the
mental patient cuts across state lines and is heard in every
section of the country. The devastating effect of mental and
emotional illness is all around us. It is reflected in delinquency, dope addiction, accidents, alcoholism, divorce, brok-
en homes, in school failure, job failure, business failure, at
high levels of national affairs and international relations.

In considering our national welfare and how to achieve
national stability, mental health, therefore, must be given
prime consideration.

Good physical health is no great asset unless accompanied
by sound mental health. A sound mind and a sound body are
needed for good living and useful citizenship.

We cannot hope to achieve success in improving the
mental health of our people unless we strike down the bigotry
and misunderstanding connected with the asylum of the past.

Therefore, all groups, private and public, must join together in the mental hospital crusade until such hospitals become houses of hope and not mere custodial places to house our so-called expendables.

Many of our state hospitals still remain a blot on our social conscience. Many are still "snake-pit" habitations for the living dead.

From the very beginning our policy has been to build factories—monstrous constructions of brick and mortar—with which to keep the patients in and the public out.

The mentally ill have been regarded by the public as something demonic, subhuman and animal-like, with words like "Batty," "Nuts," "Insane," "Balmy" and "Lunatic" characterizing American speech and the laws on our statute books. Though we have accomplished a change in public attitude, there is much work still to be done.

This is a problem of people like you and me—who grew up with the same dreams, hopes, aspirations. But something happened—they never realized their dreams. Instead, they were shunned, feared, ridiculed, ignored.

Mental illness is our number one public health problem. When we are concerned with mental health, we must be concerned with state hospitals, for eighty-five per cent of all mental health patients are in state hospitals. Yes, there are a great many mental patients in a great many mental hospitals in our country. If you were to put all the patients together in one spot, they would equal in number the population of a great city.

Our ability to shun, fear, ridicule or ignore this group is astounding. Its victims—those in hospitals and those outside hospitals—are three times more numerous than the vic-

tims of cancer and fifteen times more numerous than the victims of tuberculosis.

Each one of these patients is somebody in trouble who
could not be taken care of at home—a mother, a father, a
brother, a sister, a sweetheart, or even a child. Perhaps the
mother had acquired the forgetfulness of the aged, or the
younger brother has become a casualty of the spirit—a combat victim of life's war of stress and strain. What happens
to these people is the best gauge I know of the kind of society
we have made for ourselves.

My interest in mental health dates back three and one-
half decades ago when I was Assistant City Attorney of Minneapolis. It seemed to me then that in so many cases involving
kleptomaniacs and mental and emotional disturbances, psychiatric examinations were desirable. Ten years later, as
Municipal Judge in the same courtroom, I felt the need of a
Psychiatric Division. I secured the services of a dedicated
psychiatrist, Dr. Alexander Dumas, who conducted many
examinations for me without charge. He was later to become
the first chairman of the Governor's Mental Health Commission of Minnesota. A decade and a half later, as Governor of
Minnesota, it was only natural that one of the causes close
to my heart should be mental health. In the intervening years,
twenty of which I had been on the bench, I had seen many
tragic cases. For example, there had come to my attention
the incident of a feeble-minded boy: In the dead of winter
a fire broke out on a farm at midnight which destroyed a
large barn and all its contents of stock, fodder and farm im-
plements. That fire was the immediate cause of the death
of the father of the family following pneumonia he con-
tracted while salvaging what he could of animals and prov-
ender.

It was soon discovered that this fire was no accident. It had been innocently set by a feeble-minded boy to see what would happen. This boy was known to all the neighborhood, who tolerated his childishness without guessing its possible consequences.

The family showed no ill will toward the boy who, in his mental innocence, caused the father's death and deprived a large family of its natural provider. Instead, they resolved to commit their lives to the study and care of the mentally handicapped.

This and similar incidents had a profound effect upon me.

More than thirty-five years ago I was a student at a small school near one of our state hospitals. On free evenings I went up with my fellow students to see the "nut house." I remember how our curiosity carried us up the hill—and how our fears kept us from going beyond the gate.

About thirty years later, as Governor of Minnesota, I visited another hospital. It was my first such tour in my official capacity. A friend stopped me on the street. "Governor," he said, "I hear you are going to visit the *nut house*."

Thirty years had passed—thirty years in which psychiatry had made great strides—thirty years in which enlightened people had learned to throw away the term "insane" and to come to look on mental patients as the victims of a sickness —a sickness from which a very great number successfully recover.

Thirty years had passed — and the state hospital remained the "nut house"—an institution whose roots were still in the *asylum*. Thirty years had passed in which I, too, had had little contact with the state hospital until, as Governor, I visited the hospitals of our state.

I visited the hospitals—I visited the barns. The cows were clean, tuberculin free, well-fed, well-bedded and well-attended. The same could not be said of the patients. In the first hospital I visited, one hundred ten were in restraints; there were double food standards; there was *one* doctor and *no* psychologist for each hospital; little therapy was being administered. I couldn't sleep for several nights. Something had gone wrong—not only in Minnesota, but in many other states as well. We had learned how to discharge the atom bomb, but we had not learned how to discharge our duty to sick people.

I am going to tell you about our Minnesota campaign to revolutionize the state hospital system, not because you have not had similar problems, but because I am familiar with it.

After my visit, I concluded I could do something immediately from an administrative viewpoint. Therefore, I signed an executive order eliminating one thousand mechanical restraints. With the loyalty and cooperation of employees, not a single incident resulted of any serious consequence from this.

Then, in preparation for the next legislative session, I appointed two committees: the Governor's Mental Health Commission, consisting of some of the outstanding psychiatrists of the state who were assigned the responsibility of presenting to me a program to meet the minimum requirements of the American Psychiatric Association. I also appointed a Citizens' Mental Health Committee of fifty representative citizens who were to assist me in selling this program to the people and the legislators. Because of the fact that the mentally sick people are the lostlings of society with no lobby group to present their rights, it was necessary to enlist the support of the people in their behalf. This is a continuing requirement and here is where the Mental Health Association comes in. We were then paying approximately $1.40 per day per patient. That included all services for salaries for doctors, nurses, therapists, food, linen, drugs and other maintenance. The Governor's Mental Health Commission recommended an increase from $1.40 to $3.00 per day, or in terms of total money, an increase from fifteen million to thirty million administratively for the biennium.

With the help of the Citizens' Committee we secured first the passage of the Mental Health Policy Act, which is the Bill of Rights for the mentally ill. In its preamble it states that mental illness is a sickness to which no shame or stigma should attach.

Some of the significant provisions of this Bill of Rights for the mentally ill in Minnesota as provided in the Act are as follows:

"WHEREAS, mental illness is a sickness with respect to which there should be no stigma or shame, and

"WHEREAS, new and more effective methods and techniques of treatment and custodial care have recently been discovered, some of which have already been applied and used in the state's institutions for the mentally ill with beneficial results, and

"WHEREAS, the State of Minnesota desires to make available to said patients the newest and most effective techniques in the care and treatment for its mentally afflicted, and

"WHEREAS, the State of Minnesota recognizes the necessity of adopting a program which will furnish dignity and hope for the patient, relief from anxiety for the patient's relatives and recognition for the psychiatric worker;

"NOW, THEREFORE, BE IT ENACTED BY THE LEGIS-
LATURE OF THE STATE OF MINNESOTA:

"The measure of services hereinafter set forth are established
and prescribed as the goal of the State of Minnesota, in its
care and treatment of the mentally ill people of the state.

"Within the limits of the appropriations for the Division of
Public Institutions the Director of Public Institutions is directed in the performance of the duties imposed upon him
by the laws of this state to bring to the measure prescribed
by Section 1 hereof the care and treatment of the mentally
ill as speedily as is possible and to thereafter subject to the
paramount authority of the Legislature with respect to appropriations, maintain said standards in the care and treatment
of the mentally ill.

"The measure of services established and prescribed by Section 1 are:

"There shall be served in state hospitals a single standard
of food for patients and employees alike, which is nutritious
and palatable together with special diets as prescribed by the
medical staff thereof. There shall be a chief dietitian in the
Division of Public Institutions and at least one dietitian at
each state hospital. There shall be adequate staff and equipment for processing preparation, distribution and serving
of food.

"There shall be a staff of persons, professional and lay, sufficient in number, trained in the diagnosis, care and treatment of the mentally ill, physical illness and including religious and spiritual counsel through qualified chaplains (who
shall be in the unclassified service) adequate to take advantage of and put into practice modern methods of psychiatry,
medicine and related field.

"There shall be a staff and facilities to provide occupational
and recreational therapy, entertainment and other creative
activities as are consistent with modern methods of treatment
and well being.

"There shall be in each state hospital for the care and treatment of the mentally ill facilities for the segregation and treatment of patients who have communicable diseases.

"The Director shall provide modern and adequate psychiatric social case work services.

"The Director shall make every effort to improve the accommodations for patients so that the same shall be comfortable and attractive with adequate furnishings, clothing and supplies.

"There shall be a separate hospital for the diagnosis, care and treatment of the mentally ill who have tuberculosis which shall conform to the standards established for the diagnosis, care and treatment of physical disease. Pending construction of such separate hospital, one of the present state hospitals, or so much thereof as may be necessary, shall be set apart for the diagnosis, care and treatment of the mentally ill who have tuberculosis and shall be staffed and equipped to meet the accepted requirements of modern medicine for the care and treatment of persons afflicted with tuberculosis.

"The standards herein established shall be adapted and applied to the diagnosis, care and treatment of senile persons, inebriate persons, mentally deficient persons and epileptic persons who come within these terms as defined in Minnesota Statutes 1945, Sec. 525. 749, Subdivisions 4, 5, 6, and 7, respectively, as amended by Laws 1947, Chapter 622, and of persons who are psychopathic personalities within the definition thereof in Minnesota Statutes 1945, Sec. 526.09.

"The Director shall establish a program of detection, diagnosis and treatment of mentally or nervously ill persons and persons described in paragraph (11) hereof, and within the limits of appropriations may establish clinics and staff the same with persons specially trained in psychiatry and related fields.

"The Director of Civil Service and the Civil Service Commission may re-classify employees of the mental institutions from time to time, and assign classifications to such salary brackets as will adequately compensate personnel and reasonably assure a continuity of adequate staff.

"In addition to the chaplaincy services, provided in Sec. 3, Subd. 2, the Director of Public Institutions shall open said institutions to ministers of the Gospel to the end that religious and spiritual counsel and services are made available to the patients therein, and shall cooperate with all ministers of the Gospel in making said patients available for religious and spiritual counsel, and shall provide such ministers of the Gospel with meals and accommodations.

"Within the limits of the appropriations therefore, the Director shall establish and provide facilities and equipment for research and study in the field of modern hospital management, the causes of mental and related illness and the treatment, diagnosis and care of the mentally ill and funds provided therefore may be used to make available services, abilities and advice of leaders in those and related fields, and may provide them with meals and accommodations and compensate them for traveling expenses and services.

"There is hereby established in the Division of Public Institutions a Commissioner of Mental Health and Mental Hospitals, who shall be in the unclassified service."

We then secured appropriations to implement this law.

These appropriations were sufficient to provide for:
1. A single standard of food
2. Sufficient personnel under a 40-hour week
3. Psychiatric aides
4. Doctors
5. Nurses
6. Psychologists
7. Dietitians

8. Occupational and recreational therapy
9. Mental Health Commissioner
10. Research
11. Clinics

For those who said it costs too much money we answered: It is good economy. Through better care and treatment, sixty-five to eighty per cent of the patients are discharged. To those who said we haven't the money, we quoted Somerset Maugham who said that "if a nation loves anything more than freedom, it will lose it; if it loves money and comfort more, it will lose that, too."

We can have all the public health and all the mental health we are willing to pay for and discipline ourselves for.

The legislature doubled our appropriations, passed a very enlightened mental health policy bill, and significant program changes were made. However, I stressed then, and have repeated since, that what we proposed and what we accomplished was only the first step needed to start us on the long road ahead that in time would lead to modern mental health services.

Appropriations alone are not enough. We must also have programs and performance. One of the main problems is how to develop a program that requires years of growth and maturing—a process that is beyond the span of office of the average governor, and how to protect the program against loss of continuity and often against ruthless political attack and even retrogression. This has to be done through the citizen groups.

We are fundamentally agreed on certain things, I believe:

1. More appropriations are needed for treatment and building programs.

2. Research, training, medical services, prevention, social work and public education services are important factors in any state program.

3. The program must be under professional direction and completely free of politics.

Since growth is dependent on continuity of staff and employees, they must be protected in their tenure and exercise of professional judgment.

On the other hand, we recognize the obstacles:

1. State sources of revenue are increasingly drying up.

2. Extreme shortage of personnel on professional level.

3. We do not know the causes of many illnesses whose victims, at this time, do not respond to treatment. We must highlight the need for research. We will not find the answers to these problems today or tomorrow.

In all human relationships, better mental health will pay good dividends in happier and more prosperous lives. We think of the mental health needs in our state hospitals. That is fundamental. Over and beyond that, the problem of mental health reaches our schools, courts, correctional and welfare institutions—yes, even industry and the public services.

Mental health problems are solved on no one level, be it federal, state or local. Nor can they be solved by government alone or private action alone. They can only be solved by teamwork between the two and by a spirit that encourages—not discourages—a sound physician-patient relationship in tax-supported facilities.

Dr. Karl Menninger says, "If we can love, this is the touchstone. This is the key to the entire therapeutic program of the modern psychiatric hospital. It dominates the behavior of the staff from director to gardener. To our patient who cannot love, we must say by our actions that we do love him. We say to him, 'You can be angry if you must. We know you have had good cause. We know you are afraid of your anger. But we are not angry and you won't be either after awhile. We are your friends; those about you are all your friends. You can relax your defenses and your tensions. As you and we come to understand your life better, the warmth of love will begin to replace your present anguish and you will find yourself getting well.' "

The challenge for public psychiatry and for individuals is the translation of this—not only into therapeutic activities but into the whole field of human relations. It is your challenge. It is my challenge. It is our answer to the destructive forces in the world that seek to pit man against man.

> *"If I can keep one heart from breaking*
> *I shall not live in vain*
> *If I can ease one life the aching,*
> *Or soothe one pain,*
> *Or help one fainting robin to its nest again,*
> *I shall not live in vain."*
>
>   (Emily Dickinson)

CHAPTER III

The Hearth, The Flag and The Prayer

Many years ago, Ambassador Harvey to the Court of St. James said, "The real strength of a nation is not in its armies and navies. A schoolhouse at the crossroads is worth more than a dreadnaught by the sea. A church at the hilltop is worth more than a score of regiments. And some day the world will come to realize that there is more power and glory in 'Lead Kindly Light' than in all the fighting anthems of the world." That statement has even greater relevance today than when it was uttered, as we are involved in a great ideological struggle to determine whether we shall remain free.

A contemporary statesman, a member of the U. N., writes: "The world is out of balance. There is too much material power and not enough moral power. That is why men look ahead with fear and a sense of insecurity. No political formula, no atomic development authority, no U. N. charter, can make good the spiritual deficit. Citizens who do not attend to that in their own community, fail in their duty to themselves, their country and their God."

The great issue facing Americans in this space age is how to be strong so we can continue to be free—strong not only economically, politically and militarily, but more especially, morally and spiritually. True, we need to maintain our military strength, an effective political front, and a strong productive capacity, but it is in another area that we have our real opportunity for victory: the moral and spiritual strength of our people.

> "I know three things must ever be
> To keep a nation strong and free;
> One is a hearthstone bright and dear,
> With busy, happy loved ones near;
> One is a ready heart and hand
> To love and serve and keep the land;
> One is a worn and beaten way
> To where the people go to pray;
> As long as these are kept alive,
> Nation and people will survive.
> God keep them always everywhere—
> The hearth, the flag, the place of prayer."

Looking frankly at the record, there is cause for real concern as we realize we are not meeting these prerequisites for a strong and free nation.

How about the integrity of the home? In St. Augustine's book, "The City of God," the significance of the family is emphasized thus: "The human family constitutes the beginning and the essential element of society. Every beginning points to some end of the same nature, and every element to the perfection of the whole of which the element is a part. Thus it becomes evident that peace in society must depend upon peace in the family and the order and harmony of rulers and ruled must directly be actualized from the order and harmony arising out of creative guidance and commensurate response in the family."

It is now axiomatic in American life that the family is a sacred institution. This most sacred human relationship, ordained by God himself, is a vital part of Judaeo-Christian tradition.

It is in the home that the lessons of mutual responsibility and of self-sacrifice are learned.

In the home each individual must be accorded the opportunity to achieve physical and spiritual maturity.

The family is intrinsic to human life and society; it is an institution sanctioned by law, blessed by religion and extolled in its highest achievements by literature and art. It is impossible to exaggerate the calamities that befall a society when the home disintegrates. The cost in terms of heartbreak and human wretchedness cannot be described; the economic cost defies calculation.

Repercussions are felt in added relief loads, increased aid to dependent children and additional costs of law enforcement, including the maintenance of penal institutions. Complications are felt in recreational programs, housing facilities, mental health work—in every area of social welfare. Every other social institution, including our churches and schools, is endangered.

And where the family degenerates, thereby leading to the serious weakening of our social and moral structure, the ground is fertile for communist infiltration from within and communist attack from without.

In my opinion three factors have caused the deterioration in the home:

1. Lack of wholesome discipline.

2. Apathy and indifference on the part of parents in the important job of parenthood.

3. Lack of Christian example.

(1) Wholesome discipline and respect for authority seem to be passé. Many parents fail to realize every child craves the authority of adults. We are denying our children something very valuable when we fail to teach them that there are certain rules which, if violated, bring quick and certain punishment. Too many of our children are sophisticated and spoiled. I believe there is a necessity for the return to some of the old-fashioned discipline to teach our youth the difference between right and wrong.

(2) There is too much apathy and indifference in the discharge of parental responsibility. The job of parenthood is forced to a secondary position by many other activities. I think of Mac, the mechanic, playing ball with his young son after a hard day's work. A neighbor said, "Mac, aren't you all tired out?" "Well, certainly I'm all tired out," said Mac. "Then what on earth are you doing that for?" Mac said, "I would rather have a backache today than a heartache tomorrow!"

Then there was a little fellow who came to his dad one day and said, "Dad, let's build a playhouse out of sticks today, shall we, Dad?" The father replied, "Shucks, sonny, let's wait until we get enough money to build a real playhouse." The next day the little fellow was run over by an automobile on his way to school. In his last dying, gasping breath, he got up in a half-crouched position on the hospital cot and whispered to his dad, "We didn't get that playhouse built, did we, Dad?"

(3) There is an appalling lack of decent example. Christian example is the best guarantee for good citizenship. Greater religious emphasis is needed in the home. A place should be found in every home for the family altar. Someone has said, "Be most prayerful of your way with your children; when you are dealing with the children you are dealing with God."

"A careful man I want to be,
A little fellow follows me—
I do not dare to go astray
For fear he'll go the self-same way.

I cannot once escape his eyes,
Whate'er he sees me do he tries—
Like me he says he's going to be—
That little chap who follows me.

He thinks that I am big and fine,
Believes in every word of mine—
The base in me he must not see,
That little chap who follows me.

I must remember as I go
Thru summer's sun and winter's snow
I'm building for the years to be
That little chap who follows me."

Every child craves friendship, recognition and adventure. An essay contest was conducted in one of the schools when the students were asked to write about the greatest American. Some wrote about the Presidents—Washington, Lincoln and others; others wrote about prominent business men, religious leaders, educational leaders, labor leaders; but the boy who won first prize wrote about the man who lived next door.

The man was a new acquaintance, having just moved there two months before, but he was very kind and thoughtful to the boy—called him by his first name, permitted him to assist in washing his car, and indicated a real interest in him. There must have been a vacuum in the home life of that boy, as apparently the friendship accorded him by this new neighbor caused him to consider him the greatest American.

Then, too, every child craves recognition. I recall an incident in the Big Brother Camp which is conducted by Big Brothers on the shores of Lake Mille Lacs each summer to provide a period of free camping for underprivileged boys. A freckle-faced boy at first did not seem to be able to adapt himself to the camp life. He complained about the food, clothing, housing and recreation—nothing suited him. One day, however, one of the counsellors conceived the idea of a freckle-faced contest. The boy won first prize; he had more freckles than any boy in camp. From that time on he became the best camper! Apparently for the first time in his life he had received recognition—even the humble recognition of having more freckles than any other boy in camp.

Further, every child craves wholesome adventure. Another incident occurred when I was presiding in the Criminal Division of the Municipal Court in Minneapolis many years ago:

The Gun Squad car was called to the Northeast section of the city. It was during prohibition days. When the detectives arrived upon the scene, they found a half barrel of moonshine whisky in the basement of the home. The father was raving drunk; the mother was in an institution for the mentally ill. Upon further search of the premises they found a 5-year-old boy and a 6-year-old girl huddled together under a piece of burlap gunny sack in a dog house at the rear of the premises. Another boy, eight years of age, his life threatened by his drunken father, had run away, but returned to his home before the detectives left. I had sent the father to the workhouse on several occasions for drunkenness, for liquor in his possession, and other similar offenses. He was past fifty and almost beyond rehabilitation. The mother, as indicated, was in a mental institution.

Assuming this 8-year-old boy would have remained in that environment until he was 18 years of age and then went out on the street to rob someone—the cry would be to put him away for a long period of time, despite the fact the boy never would have had a chance for a normal home life and the opportunity to learn the difference between right and wrong. Society is in "particeps criminis" when it fails to take up the slack in a situation like this when a home breaks down and to provide a substitute type of wholesome activity for these underprivileged youngsters.

Out of the ancient Talmud comes a story of the king who had a dream. He dreamt that he saw Justice standing with a large pair of scales in her hand. On one side of the scales was located silver and gold, land, lumber and buildings. That weighed to the earth. On the other side of the scales was a nest of straw, and that side tipped to the heavens. In his dream the king saw a guardian angel approach the nest of straw and place therein a little child. Gradually that side of the scales weighed to the earth, which proved to the king that the child was the most important thing on earth. Yes, even more important than silver and gold and land and lumber and buildings. How right he was!

The second prerequisite of a strong nation is a more alert and dedicated citizenry. Many complain about the conditions of our society and yet the indifference of these people helps bring about the conditions. They are like the girl who was invited on her first date. She called her pastor to get some advice about it. He said, "If your boy friend places his hand on one shoulder, I'll not worry. If he places his hand on your other shoulder, I'll not worry, but if he places his head on your shoulder, I'll do some conscientious worrying." She had her date and came back to her pastor a couple of weeks later and he asked, "How did you get along?" "Well, Pastor, my boy friend placed his hand on one shoulder and then on the other shoulder and then, Pastor, I decided to place my head on his shoulder and let his own preacher do the worrying about the situation!"

Too often we think of the enforceable obligations of citizenship—serving on the jury, paying taxes, obeying the laws—these are of highest importance. But back of them stand the non-enforceable obligations—life itself, the art of living so that life shall be good and beautiful, and there shall be dignity and reverence for every human personality.

Now, as always, the essential ingredient in effective, vital democracy is but one thing alone—individual willingness to shoulder responsibility for conduct of government. Lose that and we are doomed to crumble and deteriorate from within.

The saving of our way of life from destruction is not a job delegated solely to a group of young men fighting and dying on the field of battle—it is a job for every citizen.

Too many citizens are afflicted with the disease of spectatoritis—sitting in the grandstand and knowing just what play ought to be called—finding fault, making scapegoats.

A working man was opening up his sandwiches one day. He came to a peanut butter sandwich and tossed it aside.

"Don't they know I don't like peanut butter sandwiches?" said he. The next sandwich was a ham sandwich. He liked ham, so he ate it. The third sandwich was another peanut butter sandwich—he tossed it aside. "Don't they know I don't like peanut butter sandwiches?" An associate workman said, "Are you married, brother?" "Now look here, don't bring my wife into this. I made those sandwiches myself!" This is the situation with many of our citizens who are always finding fault but who haven't accepted their citizenship responsibilities.

People have come to associate odious motives and practices with politics. Politics is the art of making government work. It is the machinery by which society makes its moral decisions. The story is told of the sage and the cynic: the cynic came to the wise old man with his fists closed and asked, "What have I got in my hands?" The wise man responded, "A bird." The cynic then asked, "Is it dead or alive?" thinking surely he would trap the old man, for if the sage responded, "Alive," the cynic would crush the bird to death in his hands, and if he responded, "Dead," the cynic would open his hands and allow the bird to fly away, proving in any event that the wise man was wrong; but the sage responded, "Just as you will, my son, just as you will." And so we get just as bad government as we are willing to stand for and just as good government as we are willing to fight for.

The Christian in government must dedicate himself to a program that places human values first. As Christ was most concerned with children and unfortunates, so must the Christian politician see that government invests generously in education, health and general welfare of youth. He must fight for humane care of the mentally ill and other fellow human beings in need of a helping hand. He must set an example of self-discipline and wholesome respect for law and order. He must work to put Christianity into practice by striving to foster and protect the heritage of citizenship for all of every race, creed, color of skin and national origin.

During my first administration as Governor of Minnesota in 1947, I came to appreciate what Christian people can do for good government when they are alerted to their responsibilities. I was fighting for the adoption of the Anti-Slot Machine Act to eliminate eight thousand slot machines and an eight million dollar racket that had existed in Minnesota. It was a rugged battle and we took a lot of abuse. At first the outcome was in doubt, but when the church people finally became aroused, they became real fighting crusaders and we were successful in securing the passage of the Act and the eight thousand slot machines left Minnesota overnight. It indicates that good government can be had if Christian people are willing to fight hard enough for it.

During the days when considerable abuse came my way because I was trying to enforce the laws on the statute books, when there was a discussion at a certain meeting I used to quote an incident concerning prenatal influence: A young man made the statement that he did not believe in prenatal influence. "Why," he said, "when my mother was carrying me, she rushed across the floor with a bunch of phonograph records in her arms and tripped over something, and smash went the records in hundreds of pieces! But," he continued, "it didn't affect me—affect me—affect me!"

The most important prerequisite, however, for a strong and free nation is that there should be a worn and beaten way to where the people go to pray. Congress has passed many important laws in the past few years, but one of the most significant acts, in my opinion, was the unanimous passage of a resolution establishing a meditation room in the Capitol. Without ostentation or blare of trumpet, a room was provided, with no emphasis, of course, upon any creed or faith, where the distinguished legislative leaders of our nation might go to receive guidance and strength from above. This act demonstrated that our legislative leaders recognized their inability in and of their own strength to resolve the difficult problems which face us. This should give us real comfort in our hour of trial.

Our nation was founded by men of faith. Thomas Jefferson, who wrote in the Declaration of Independence the immortal principles with which we are all so familiar, warned us, "Our liberties are the gift of God. If we do not nourish them, we may lose them." George Washington, who unsheathed his sword and led the Colonial Armies to victory to put these principles into practice, warned from his deathbed, "Beware of the man who attempts to inculcate morality without religion." Benjamin Franklin, who signed the treaty of peace in behalf of the American colonies that guaranteed to them these rights forever, stressed the necessity of prayer and emphasized if this nation did not place its trust in God, it could not endure.

At a very perilous time in our nation's history, Abraham Lincoln, the Great Emancipator, just before Thanksgiving Day in 1863, urged the people to get down on their knees in penitence, asking forgiveness as he said, "We have been the recipients of the choicest bounties of heaven. We have been preserved these many years in peace and prosperity. We have grown in numbers, wealth and power as no other nation has ever grown, but we have forgotten God. We have forgotten the gracious hand which preserved us in peace and multitude and enriched and strengthened us and we have vainly claimed in the deceitfulness of our hearts that all these blessings were produced by some superior wisdom and virtue of our own. Intoxicated by unbroken success, we have become too self-sufficient to feel the necessity of religion and preserving grace, too proud to pray to the God that made us. It behooves us then to humble ourselves before the offended power, to confess our national sins and to pray for forgiveness."

Our freedom comes from God and it will be under God that we will continue to be free.

Our free way of life was developed by men and women of deep religious faith. America has always been conscious of the need for religion. The founders of our republic were sincerely and profoundly men who looked to God for guidance.

The western world must do more than build up armaments and stockpile raw materials. As necessary as is military defense in this period of history, we delude ourselves if we think our many-billion dollars a year military budget will save us. We must act with every spiritual resource at our command if we are to win this struggle. Millions of people who are now indifferent to God are unconsciously giving aid, comfort and help to the communists. A moral breakdown is fast undermining America. We are being seriously threatened from a collapse from inner decay.

Headlines tell only a part of the story of increase in murders and crimes of violence, juvenile delinquency, sex promiscuity, narcotics, graft, corruption and apathy on the part of most, except evil-doers. Despite encouragement from increased church attendance in recent years, approximately fifty per cent of our people still remain unchurched. Although United States Sunday School enrollments are at an all-time high (well above the 32,000,000 mark) yet 27,000,000 other American children and youth receive little or no church training and of the 1,000,000 children who, each year, get into trouble with the law, the vast majority have no record of regular religious instruction.

As in the public schools, Sunday church schools, in many cases, are overcrowded and handicapped by a lack of teachers. As a Christian nation, we cannot afford to let a single child go without his spiritual heritage. Although our stewardship programs and parish work activities have been stepped up in many of our churches, we are still lagging far behind in the amount we appropriate for such work. We spend a far larger sum for horse race betting and for liquor today than we spend for our church Sunday schools and humanitarian causes.

Our religion and democracy are so strong they can never be conquered by open attack. They can only succumb to indifference and neglect. Arnold Toynbee said, "All civilizations which have been destroyed, have destroyed themselves and that even where a civilization's downfall has apparently come from outside forces, external pressures merely reveal the internal weaknesses which antedated the crisis. The fall of the Roman Empire was due largely to internal corruption and in more modern history we note the corruption and lack of respect for law in the French nation was even more dangerous to the French than the German troops on the other side of the Maginot Line."

A short time ago in Washington, a prominent businessman stated at a public meeting, "Our American way of life

—that splendid, tough, permanent revolution inaugurated by our founding fathers—is a dead, flat thing without God for a basis." He further emphasized that the current defense program is not enough. "Add up the efforts expended in economic and military aid, and is this the totality that is America?" he asked. He asserted it was not, and that America was something finer, deeper and nobler than economics and the military. "The real America is a religious nation; let's go back to it."

And so,

> *"I know three things must ever be*
> *To keep a nation strong and free;*
> *One is a hearthstone bright and dear,*
> *With busy, happy loved ones near;*
> *One is a ready heart and hand*
> *To love and serve and keep the land;*
> *One is a worn and beaten way*
> *To where the people go to pray.*
> *As long as these are kept alive,*
> *Nation and people will survive.*
> *God keep them always everywhere—*
> *The hearth, the flag, the place of prayer."*

CHAPTER IV

All God's Children

At the time the country commemorated the seventy-fifth birthday of the distinguished poet and philosopher, Carl Sandburg, he penned these lines:

"There is only one horse on the earth,
And his name is all horses;
There is only one bird in the air,
And his name is all wings;
There is only one fish in the sea,
And his name is all fins;
There is only one man in the world,
And his name is all men;
There is only one woman in the world,
And her name is all women;
There is only one child in the world,
And the child's name is all children;
There is only one Maker in the world,
And His children cover all the earth,
And they are named all God's children."

Citizens on a Washington pilgrimage come from different parts of the United States and from different religious denominations but all as God's children to rededicate and re-

consecrate themselves to the spiritual heritage which has
made America great. The Washington Pilgrimage is a broad
religious movement that draws its strength from all faiths.
They have come here because they recognize the fact that we
cannot take for granted that our religious heritage will endure.

When Benjamin Franklin came out of the Constitutional
Convention, it is related that a lady asked him, "What shall
it be, Mr. Franklin, a monarchy or a republic?" Mr. Franklin responded, "A republic, if you can keep it." To keep our
republic we must keep our religious faith strong. Many have
merely a hazy remembrance of the tenets of the American
system—the Bill of Rights and some phrases from the Constitution or the Declaration of Independence but forget the
fundamental truths upon which the tenets are based. These
truths are the law and the will of God. Only if these are understood and espoused can evil be defeated.

The freedom that the colonists sought was the right to
seek grace through a personal relationship with God, free
from the intervention of other men, the right to human dignity
based on this relationship rather than on man-made standards, and the moral responsibility and brotherhood arising
from this relationship. It was to gain these rights for themselves and for the generations to follow that they staked their
lives and their fortunes and forged the American political,
economic and social system as set forth in the Declaration
of Independence, the Constitution of the United States and
the Bill of Rights.

In Sandburg's novel, "Remembrance Rock," retired Supreme Court Justice Windom had constructed a remembrance
rock in the garden of his home. There he had reverently
placed containers of earth from the principal battlefields of

the nation. Justice Windom was wont to retire to remembrance rock for a renewal of his faith. When he passed away his grandson noticed these words written on remembrance rock: "The terrific obstacles that faced our people in the early beginnings of our nation when the republic seemed to hang in balance—these must be remembered. To lose them is to lose the republic. Nations go down when they forget where they came from and when they become satisfied with themselves." Today we need to retire to our remembrance rock for dedication, faith and prayer. For we are participants in an unparalleled struggle for the minds and souls of men. Arrayed on one side are the spiritually barren ideologies which endeavor to uproot the spiritual foundations of our society. On the other side are the cherished spiritual concepts and religious values without which our society would soon pass into oblivion.

The nature of the struggle in which these contrasting ideologies are engaged is illustrated in the statement of Lenin: "It does not matter a jot if three-quarters of the human race perish: the important thing is that the remaining one-quarter be Communists." The contrast to this philosophy we find in St. John, thirteenth chapter, verses 34 and 35: "A new commandment I give unto you, that ye love one another; as I have loved you, that ye also love one another. By this shall all men know that ye are my disciples, if you have love one to another."

Arnold Toynbee said, "All civilizations which have been destroyed, have destroyed themselves and that even where a civilization's downfall has apparently come from outside forces, external pressures merely reveal the internal weaknesses which antedated the crisis. The fall of the Roman Empire was due largely to internal corruption and in more modern history we note the corruption and lack of respect for law in the French nation was even more dangerous to the French than the German troops on the other side of the Maginot Line."

Fortunately for America and for the world, there seems to be developing a spiritual renaissance. The big event of our age is a spiritual something that has been growing in the hearts of men. Even secular organizations recognize the necessity of religion. The American Legion and the Fraternal Order of Eagles during the past year have stressed the necessity of religious emphasis in the lives of their members. On every side one hears, "America's problem is a spiritual one." Because, despite our material resources, we Americans are searching for confidence, conviction and hope. It is not the first time America has needed hope. The men and women of 1776 needed the same thing. Their strength was the inner assurance that comes from a living faith in God. Our free way of life was developed by men and women of deep religious faith.

At a Prayer Breakfast recently held in the Nation's Capitol, former President Eisenhower said: "Without a continuation of basic principles on which our nation was founded our system of government cannot endure. Only a people strong in Godliness is a people strong enough to overcome tyranny and make themselves free and others free. . . . You can't explain free government in any other terms than religious. The founding fathers had to refer to the Creator in order to make their revolutionary experiment make sense; it was because all men are endowed by their Creator with certain inalienable rights that men could dare to be free. They wrote their religious faith into our founding document, stamped their trust in God on the faces of their coins and currency and put it boldly at the base of our institutions. And when they drew up their bold Bill of Rights, where did they put Freedom of Worship? First, in the cornerstone position. That was no accident. But the paramount issue of the day is this: Do we still have religion in the cornerstone position in our hearts?"

This job of building a better country is not only for the President of the United States. It is a job for every individual citizen. It means the acceptance of individual responsibilities. The story is told of a young German who went to the German philosopher, Goethe, to get his autograph. In addition to writing his autograph, Goethe penned this important bit of philosophy, "Let everyone sweep the broom clean in front of his own door and the whole world will be clean." The world will be reformed only as the consecration process takes place in the hearts of individuals.

Bonaro Overstreet has said:

> "You say the little efforts that I make will do no good,
> They will never prevail to tip the heavy scale
> Where justice hangs in balance,
> I do not think I ever thought they would,
> But I am prejudiced beyond debate
> In favor of my right to choose which side
> Shall feel the stubborn ounces of my weight."

This nation needs the stubborn ounces of weight of every Christian.

> "What makes a city great and strong?
> Not architecture's graceful strength,
> Not factories' extended length,
> But men who see the civic wrong,
> And give their lives to make it right,
> And turn its darkness into light.

What makes a city man can love?
  Not things that charm the outward sense,
  Not gross display of opulence,
But right that wrong cannot remove,
And truth, that faces civic fraud
And smites it, in the name of God.

This is a city that shall stand,
  A light upon a nation's hill,
  A voice that evil cannot still,
A source of blessing to the land;
Its strength not brick, nor stone, nor wood,
But Justice, Love and Brotherhood."

CHAPTER V

Molding Minds

The primary purpose of Education Week is to focus public attention on the schools, to acquaint the public with the work of the schools, with their ideals, achievements and needs. Our schools are supported through public funds and it is only fair that sometime during the year the public should have the privilege of visiting the schools and obtaining a first-hand knowledge of what the schools are accomplishing. This is exactly what American Education Week affords. It brings the patrons of the schools and the general public into closer contact with our educational system.

Public education, along with the home and the church, forms the very foundation of American democracy. Freedom and representative government can survive only in the hands of an enlightened people.

Education is made effective by a continuation of public interest and the efforts of the school personnel. The public and the teachers must know each other if they are to work together.

Teachers and citizens generally then should use American Education Week to become better acquainted with each other.

Through the interest that will be stimulated during Education Week will come new strength for education. Only a deep-seated public interest will guarantee schools the quality and competence needed to do their part in keeping America free and strong.

A poet once said that "the proper study of mankind is man." Never has this truth been more apparent than today.

Modern man is in a peculiar and dangerous predicament. He has given himself to enthusiastic study of the problems and the mystery of science. His efforts have been rewarded by a success that, at times, bewilders him. With rapid thrusts he has rolled back the frontiers of science and technology. In two centuries he has made more progress in the discovery and application of natural law than was achieved in the previous two thousand years. Slowly he is coming to realize that in his possession now is knowledge which, if used unwisely, can bring about the destruction of civilization.

The crucial question of our time is whether a horrible catastrophe can be averted. The answer to that depends upon whether another world war can be avoided. And the abolishment of war can be accomplished only if man can succeed in pushing back another frontier—the frontier in human relations. The great need of the hour is for human engineers who will work with the energy and genius that has brought achievement for our mechanical engineers, our chemical engineers, our aeronautical engineers and other researchers in the field of science.

The Golden Age of man seems sadly lacking! Civilization is threatened not so much by nuclear fission as by a lack of knowledge of man himself. No one is more aware of the situation than the scientist. The American Association for the

Advancement of Science has stressed that research must now be concentrated upon "human science" so that civilization may be saved. We still flounder in the quest for the simple formulas which can bring world peace at the conference table, agreement in the factory and workshop and can tie our families together.

Ominous shadows of greed and passion hang heavy over a world which lives in fear that a rival nation may be the first to push the button or drop the bomb that will touch off the flames and horror of an atomic and germ war. Some people indulge in wishful thinking for miraculous research to provide a mental gadget to straighten out our human relations. Of course this is a futile hope! Our problem is ourselves and it cannot be solved so easily. Look for no miracle! Only enlightenment in human relations can eliminate the fears which cloud the lives of mankind.

What shall be the role of the public school in this endeavor to improve our human engineering and build a better world? I believe it must be a role based on the realization that the public schools are the very sinews of our democracy. We must depend upon them as one of the primary sources of strength for our way of life—which means freedom to worship God according to one's conscience, freedom of speech and discussion, freedom of political expression and action, and freedom to live one's personal life with liberty under the law.

Universal education extending beyond the elementary level has long been an American idea—or perhaps I should say *ideal*. We have a long way to go before all the youth of the nation are given an equal opportunity to receive the benefits of a good education. From the beginning of our history there has been an effort by citizens with vision to make free schools available to all American youth.

Yet our ideal has not been attained in education. Several million American school children from the ages of six to fifteen are not in school. Poorest schools spend less than $100 per classroom unit and best-supported schools $6,000 per classroom unit. Several million persons over twenty-five years of age have not gone beyond the fourth grade.

This year the schools are facing the "Battle of the Bulge" in enrollment, as more students have crowded into the nation's classrooms than ever before. This has required double shifts and the hiring of halls and other premises in order to accommodate the students.

There is a need for two hundred fifty thousand new classrooms. Thirteen and one-half billion dollars must be spent in the 1950's in elementary and secondary school plants.

We know that many of the schools in our nation are housed in dilapidated buildings. Equipment is outmoded. Textbooks are found to be old and obsolete. Another sign of weakness in our system of public education is the fact that three hundred fifty thousand qualified teachers left the classrooms of the nation during the war years to accept more remunerative positions. Although the situation is improving in some fields, a serious shortage of qualified teachers still exists, especially in elementary education.

The truth of the matter, I believe, is that America must be willing to allot more of her income to education than she has in the past. Good schools cost money. I submit it is a wise investment. Consider the statistics on the expenditure of national income. It is estimated that we spend only two and two-tenths per cent of our national income for education, but we spend four and nine-tenths per cent on alcoholic beverages and three and four-tenths per cent on horse race betting alone. Certainly our nation can afford to spend at least as much for education as for alcoholic beverages and horse race betting. Rather we should spend many times more for education.

The first need of our schools lies in securing an adequate number of well-prepared teachers. We must continue to progress in our efforts to attract capable young men and women to the teaching profession through fair salaries, adequate housing facilities, retirement privileges and attractive working conditions. We must provide them with adequate equipment, books and buildings.

Most important is the teacher. As someone has said, "as the teacher is, so is the child; as the child is, so is tomorrow." That statement should remind us of the vital role of the teacher.

A second challenge to our schools lies in developing a curriculum that will do a better job of teaching children how to live together. We must improve vastly our efforts to show children the importance of living together harmoniously in our homes, on our own streets, in our communities, our state and the nation, or we can make no claim to provide moral leadership to the world.

Schools must seek out new methods and techniques to guard the hearts and minds of children from the poisons of bigotry and intolerance. There is no intolerance in the heart of a child. That is, there is none there until it has been planted by the words and examples of intolerant adults. The schools of the nation must be ever vigilant in this effort to stamp out prejudice.

There is a need for schools that give more concern to the moral questions. It is not enough for our schools to develop intellectual literacy. They must do more than bring a mastery of language, figures and historical dates. They must also educate for social, moral and spiritual literacy or be considered a failure in preparing the child to meet the challenges of these times. Though we must insure separation of Church and State as provided for in the Constitution, it does not mean that it is necessary to have an irreligious atmosphere prevail in the schools.

Dr. D. Campbell Wyckoff, Chairman, Department Religious Education, New York University, has said: "The country's schools, with few exceptions, throughout the years had recognized that sectarian neutrality must not mean hostility to religion or to the churches.

"The purpose of American education is rooted in the religious faith of the Jewish-Christian tradition underlying our whole structure. Behind the need for maintaining sectarian impartiality is a positive need to maintain the moral and religious truth upon which our national life has been built.

"Especially in critical times like ours, the character of the future citizen depends on friendly mutual understanding even among institutions that must remain forever separate.

"The aim of education is not to produce children and youth who are merely informed and skilled but without moral and religious commitments. The aim of education is rather to produce the citizen of deep and intelligent convictions. This is the heart of the public school's task and without question, involves implications that are moral and spiritual in character."

Better human engineering will also come as we give added emphasis to the importance of teaching our children how to think for themselves instead of passively accepting the statements of teacher or of textbook. Teachers should constantly encourage discussion, debate and questions. Let your chief concern be to teach youth to think—not what to think! Youth will find the right road and the right answer if we adults will provide guidance which encourages independent thought, an inquiring attitude and initiative.

In these times the school is also challenged to do a better job in strengthening the home as our basic institution. Of course the school is no substitute for the home. But modern living has brought grave dangers to the home and family. Greater stress and conflict in the home is indicated in the increasing number of divorces over the past fifty years. In 1890 there was one divorce to every sixteen marriages; in 1910, one divorce to every eleven marriages; in 1940, one divorce to six marriages. Today, it is estimated that one out of every three marriages end in divorce and many authorities predict the situation will get worse—unless we do something about it.

What can the school do to strengthen the institutions of home and family? Church, school, and parents must join hands in providing youth with a knowledge of family and marriage that will enable them to succeed as homemakers and parents.

All girls should have a chance to study home economics before leaving school. They should leave the secondary school with at least some knowledge of cooking, sewing, interior decorating, child care and other subjects vital in the creation of family life.

Moreover, more attention should be paid to the whole phase of mental health. A doctor, in a speech at the Menninger Foundation, stressed this need as follows: "Time is being spent teaching children multiplication and division of fractions, rules of grammar and how the Indians build their tepees, but practically nothing is being done to teach children what happens when personal ambitions run too far ahead of the individual's capacity for performance, or how to better understand and deal with the people they must get along with in the world."

He advocates that teachers receive instruction in principles of mental health. He recommends that every school have a workable system of collecting pertinent information about each individual child so that his needs may be quickly discovered and provided for as he passes from one teacher or school to another. He adds that academic education is supposed to be preparation for life and yet we are allowing children to grow up haphazardly with respect to the laws of mental health.

Along with a better understanding of mental health goes the need for an appreciation of the importance of wholesome recreation to the development of a well-adjusted personality. Children must be taught the importance of forming good play and recreation habits, which will aid the health of body and mind.

To fit our children for the challenges of modern life, I believe our schools must also do more to provide vocational guidance. Guidance deserves to be termed the keystone of the art of public education. More attention should be given to the assessing of the capabilities of the student as he moves through the educational process. Only through guidance will the school be able to help the boy or girl find the kind of satisfying employment to correspond with ambitions and abilities.

Another phase of human engineering to which our schools should give greater attention is the matter of citizenship. Teachers, I believe, should set an example by taking an active part in public affairs. They should develop in youth an appreciation of the responsibility of voting and maintaining an interest in civic activities.

These are perilous times in which we live and our democracy must be developed to the fullest of its potentialities. This means that our schools must be strong, if we are to survive.

Our schoolteachers, then, are truly in the forefront of this fight to improve our human engineering and preserve our free way of life.

I like the philosophy expressed by a teacher, Anna R. Maskel. Listen to her words: "I am just a sixth-grade country schoolteacher, but to me is entrusted the greatest wealth of our community—the minds and hearts of its children. I feel the sacredness of my trust—a trust which I can best fulfill by nurturing within my classroom the microcosm of a better world, a world where personal dignity will be respected and where everyone will be given not only the opportunity, but also the incentive to make the highest possible use of his endowments.

"To match the strides of growing youth, I, too, must constantly replenish my mind and spirit; and in the process of striving to become a better teacher, my own personal life is enriched intellectually, emotionally and aesthetically—I say aesthetically because intimate association with children adds beauty and loveliness to all life's experiences!"

America's great need is for teachers who have the high spirit and vision of this outstanding educator and for enlightened citizens who are willing to support an educational system that will produce the kind of citizens needed for tomorrow's leadership.

CHAPTER VI

Building Bridges

No nation can rise higher than its dedication to the cause of youth. The future of the nation will be shaped by the job we do in preparing youth physically, mentally and spiritually for adulthood.

The critical days in which we live bring to us adults the urgency to give the best in ourselves to the cause of youth. One hundred years from now it will not matter much what material resources we possessed, what our bank account was, or the kind of house we lived in, but it will matter whether we had any influence in the lives of youth.

We can help change the world by being important in the lives of boys and girls. If we can play some part in shaping their lives, if we can assist them along the road of noble character and constructive citizenship, we can help shape the history of tomorrow.

For centuries Western society has acted on the belief that any person—whether adult or child—who breaks the law does so solely because he consciously or wilfully prefers evil to good. This belief, in so many cases, underlies our criminal law and its administration with the result that it has relied on punishment to fit the crime and on the threat of such punishment to keep people on good behavior. Of course, the theory has not worked out in practice. If severity of punishment could control behavior, we should have long since had a paradise of good citizenship. We should not now be worried about delinquency and crime.

Deeper insight into the multitude of complicated factors that lead human beings to behave as they do helps us to see why punishment fails to adequately protect society. Punishment deals only with symptoms and not with causes. We must stress the efficacy of prevention. There are many pressures that contribute to juvenile delinquency. We should seek to determine the pressures which cause the trouble and to remove them in a friendly and understanding spirit.

The odds against youth these days are many—such as adult irresponsibility, physical and mental handicaps, crowded tenement areas, insufficient recreational opportunities, underequipped schools—but the greatest handicap of all is lack of religious emphasis in the life of the child.

Juvenile delinquency will decrease in the proportion to the extent that we intensify our efforts in religious education. To teach our children knowledge is not enough—we must equip them with more than social and intellectual literacy. More important is the development of moral and spiritual literacy. Fundamentally, of course, the job belongs to the home. There never will be a substitute for a good, decent home with parents who really care and who understand the exalted nature of the job of parenthood. But many of the homes in the nation are breaking down through separation and divorce and through lack of proper discipline, companionship and example. Society hasn't done its full part where homes have failed to do the job.

Every child craves and needs friendship, recognition, adventure and good example. If the child does not get these prerequisites in a constructive way, he will get them from negative and bad influences.

Youth Conservation programs established in some of the states should be encouraged and intensified. These programs should encompass diagnostic facilities as well as preventive programs. Every state has a responsibility to set up uniform diagnostic services under a Youth Commission so that each child will be considered individually—with treatment directed according to what is best for the rehabilitation of the child.

States also need prevention services in helping communities set up coordinating councils which have as their function research, community education, strengthening existing youth services, and pilot projects.

The emphasis in our plans for youth must be on community action. Someone once said that "the test of a good community is the provision it makes for the welfare of children of all creeds, color, races and nationalities, without regard to financial or social status of the parents." State agencies can guide, assist and encourage the local community, but in the final analysis it is up to the people of the local community to carry out the plans for youth and thus meet the test of a good community.

With this philosophy as its guide, Minnesota, in 1947, passed its Youth Conservation Act—one of the wisest investments the state has ever made. The Act is based on three fundamental beliefs:

The first is that to control delinquency and crime more effectively we must remove the causes. This approach can be likened to that of a farmer who was once shown a gnarled and twisted tree. He was asked for an opinion as to the cause of its distortion and immediately he replied, "Someone must have stepped on it when it was young."

The second fundamental belief on which Minnesota's Youth Conservation program is based is that major responsibility for prevention and correction must remain with the community. It is believed that this is not only desirable, but inescapable. Effective prevention must be done in the community. That prevention activity is a product of the moral climate, values, customs, understanding, organization, services and vitality of the community itself. As for the rescue of children who have already become delinquent, this, too, can for the most part only be accomplished by the community. Correction involves such steps as detection, arrest, detention, diagnosis, trial or hearing, and treatment—including probation, placement in a foster home, institutionalization, parole, and supervision. All the steps that affect the great majority of youthful offenders take place locally. Even the small percentage committed to state training schools under the program soon return and depend upon the community for successful re-absorption.

The third fundamental belief upon which the program is founded is that prevention and correction are often parts of the same process, and if maximum effectiveness is the goal, they cannot be divorced. For example, good work by police, probation or parole officers with children who get into trouble requires close cooperation with the schools for the adjustment of these children and for removal of factors in the school that may contribute to their maladjustment; such removal in turn will prevent other children from becoming delinquent.

To carry out this new emphasis, Minnesota created the Youth Conservation Commission to: (1) Rehabilitate delinquent children and convicted offenders under twenty-one years of age committed to it by the courts; (2) Make prehearing investigations and provide probation supervision for all juvenile courts not having their own county probation officers; and (3) Help local communities reduce and prevent delinquency and improve all services to children.

The role of the Youth Conservation Commission, then, is not to take over responsibility from the community. Its purpose is rather to supplement local resources where necessary and to furnish communities the assistance needed in analyzing and coordinating their correctional and preventive services to youngsters.

Every community can be shown how to take care of nearly all its delinquent youngsters. However, there are likely to be a few so emotionally disturbed or otherwise troublesome as to require removal from their homes and treatment by specially trained personnel. So the first function of the Youth Conservation Commission is to be responsible for the care of and the attempt to rehabilitate all delinquent children and convicted offenders under twenty-one years of age whom the courts feel cannot be dealt with locally. For this purpose the Commission is directed to set up reception centers where experts in many fields can study each child carefully and determine the causes that led him into trouble. After making this study, the Commission decides upon the treatment which will do most to rehabilitate the youthful offender and has full power to carry out the treatment prescribed. The Commission can send the youth to an institution for a period, send him home on probation, arrange for some special treatment, or do anything else that might help him.

A second function of the Commission is to provide probation services to many of the counties, for few of the non-metropolitan areas have a sufficient case load to justify a full-time trained probation officer. Yet good probation services are perhaps the most effective single tool in rescuing children from delinquency. Thus the Commission has an important assignment in helping meet this need.

Probation workers of the Commission go out from day to day as the youngsters are returned home to help them make adjustments. Resources of whole communities are organized in many instances to give an erring boy a welcome and the all-important feeling that he is accepted and a part of the community.

Boys and girls who get into some difficulty and leave home under a cloud are re-established in wholesome pursuits by this method in case after case. Often just a little human kindness, just a little help at this crucial period is sufficient. In community after community there have been troublesome youngsters who have been set upon a new path.

The third major function of the Commission is educational rather than administrative. The responsibility falls upon the state to provide help and guidance to communities in improving the youth services they have and in adding essential new services in order to do a better job in rescuing children who have become delinquent and in preventing delinquency. The responsibility to give this assistance has been given in the main to the Commission.

In fulfilling this function, the Commission has carried on a program to encourage communities to study their own resources in recreation, health, law enforcement and other services which affect the welfare of youth. The Commission has shown communities how they can reorganize and strengthen existing services, where this can be helpful, to provide more effectively for the needs of their boys and girls. Where the present services are found to be inadequate, the Commission has encouraged all forces in the community to join hands in a cooperative effort to provide the new facilities needed. Minnesota's State Youth Commission and other state departments have joined hands with local officials and citizens in many communities in conducting a local survey of youth services, which has helped these communities to see their needs and develop ways to meet them. To put this kind of cooperative effort on a permanent basis, the Commission has helped organize many local Youth Commissions and has assisted the formation of other similar groups.

Specific responsibility for prevention activities of the Commission falls mainly upon a team of field representatives, juvenile control consultants, and recreation consultants —directed by the chief of the division of prevention and parole. The team provides consultant services on community organization for prevention, on juvenile control, and on recreation; conducts community surveys of youth services; and conducts state and regional workshops on youth services.

Most communities desire to do the best they can for their children. To capitalize on this interest, the Commission began its prevention services by offering aid to those desiring to organize local Youth Commissions.

You may wonder about the make-up and purpose of such local Commissions. They are coordinating bodies to provide a means of bringing together all the agencies and citizens who are interested in serving youth. Typical membership includes representatives of schools, police, local government, churches, youth groups such as 4-H clubs and Boy Scouts, women's organizations, service and fraternal clubs, labor unions, and business organizations. Working together on the Commissions, these representatives can look at the total needs of youth in the community and the resources for meeting them and discover gaps.

In addition, the Commission has assisted in the organization of Youth Councils in some of our communities and more are in process of formation. They are made up of boys and girls from young people's organizations and they meet to plan and coordinate group activities. They have representation on the Youth Commissions so that youth may have a voice in community plans for its own welfare.

Let us look at a few examples of results produced thus far by the community surveys and the local commissions. Here is one city that now has a Youth Canteen and a Vocational Guidance program at its high school and an improved law enforcement program because the survey revealed these basic needs. Here is another community that, through the survey, found its leisure-time activities for youth to be inferior. Now it has a Recreation Committee and a director of recreation hard at work on an expanded program. A third city conducted a survey to find more volunteer leadership for a better youth program. Other communities found that the health of their children was not being properly checked and now have physical examination programs, with means of assistance found for necessary treatment of children when the families lack money to pay for it. Through these and many other ways, the prevention program is helping the communities to better serve youth.

To further stimulate interest and organization for youth, the state of Minnesota has held statewide Governor's Youth Conferences. These conferences had an attendance of from

1000 to 2000 people from all parts of the state. The Youth Conservation Commission served as secretariat for these conferences. Out of these conferences have come many valuable recommendations and clearer understanding of the needs of the young people of Minnesota. Many of our worthwhile legislative recommendations have been formulated in the hard-working committees of these conferences.

Our first Youth Conference set forth "The Seven Basic Needs of Children and Youth" as follows:

"Consistent and firm support from the home, supplemented by school, church and other institutions to build healthy interpersonal relationships through which security, love and acceptance may be achieved.

"Opportunity to assume increasing responsibility commensurate with age and ability which will result in the satisfactions of achievement.

"Opportunity to develop skills of living which will lead to more adequate adjustment to a changing world.

"Adequate provision for all essentials to physical health.

"Equal educational opportunities consistent with native endowment and interest.

"Active participation in community living through constructive work and play.

"Encouragement toward a rich and meaningful spiritual life."

Guided by these seven basic needs, Minnesota is striving to chart the way to better services for youth. Out of the conferences and the continuing work of its committees have come valuable recommendations for communities and for legislative action. For example, the Youth Conference recommended that a forestry camp be made a part of our Youth Conservation program. The Legislature appropriated funds for it at a later session.

The guiding thought of one of the statewide Governor's Youth Conferences was this: "If all the youth of America could speak to us, they would speak with one voice and say, 'We are the future, for in us there lies what through the ages this land shall be. Yet what we are is what you are to us. We are the question to which you make reply.' "

To answer that question, we must give our best in serving youth. That is our most crucial challenge in the world today. I am confident that out of this great conference you will develop many worthy plans and receive renewed inspiration to better help the youth of the nation.

Let us be guided by the philosophy of "The Bridge Builder":

> "An old man going a lone highway
> Came at the evening, cold and gray,
> To a chasm vast and deep and wide.
> The old man crossed in the twilight dim—
> The sullen stream had no fear for him.
> But he paused, when safe on the other side
> And built a bridge to span the tide.
>
> 'Old Man,' said a fellow pilgrim near,
> 'You are wasting your time in building here.
> Your journey ends at the close of day
> And you will never again pass this way;
> You've crossed the chasm deep and wide,
> Why build this bridge at eventide?'
>
> The traveler raised his old gray head,
> 'Good friend, in the path I've come,' he said,
> 'There followeth after me today

A youth whose feet must pass this way.
This chasm has been as naught to me,
But to that fair youth may a pitfall be.
He, too, must cross in the twilight dim.
Good friend, I'm building the bridge for him.' "

CHAPTER VII

There Is a Destiny That Makes Us Brothers

We salute the National Association for Retarded Children. Ten years ago it was my privilege, as Governor of Minnesota, to speak at the organizational meeting of the Association in the city of Minneapolis and to install their first officers. At that first meeting, there were forty-two delegates, representing local associations in fourteen states.

A masterful statement of purposes emanated from the labors of that first convention. These were parents with a purpose—no money, no precedent, no policy to follow. The officers and directors in most instances were strangers to one another—but strangers with a common goal: To help all retarded children and their parents.

When I installed the officers on that memorable Saturday night September 30, 1950, among other things, I said, "Our great democracy can be measured best by what it does for the least of its little children." That has even greater relevancy in this space age.

What a different picture today! It is now one of the most powerful voluntary health organizations in America, with 800 local associations representing forty-nine states. Its membership rolls have swelled to more than 60,000—quite an increase over the forty-two individuals who convened in Minneapolis just a decade ago.

In the State of Minnesota, there is a strong Association for Mentally Retarded which, with many other Associations over the country, has been busy gathering information for presentation to an interim Commission studying the needs of the retarded.

This organization came into being and grew so rapidly because of the desperate need for a strong voice for the five million mentally retarded children and adults who could not speak for themselves.

In 1950, the care of the mentally retarded had reached a very low point. As against the hopeful trend of the first quarter of the century, the very size of the problem led to a feeling of defeatism and despair among legislative and welfare leaders. The high post-war birth rate, combined with remarkable reductions in infant mortality, produced a larger number of young, severely mentally retarded children than at any time in our history. While the majority of these more handicapped youngsters were potentially trainable in social adjustment and manual skills, the overburdened public schools rejected them.

A short decade ago there were in this country millions of forgotten children—the mentally retarded. Due to ignorance and the erroneous belief that their future was hopeless, they were shunted aside. We were not even prepared or willing to provide custodial care, even though commitment to an institution was the only answer the medical profession then had for these children.

Distraught and despairing parents who turned to physicians for guidance were invariably told to place their retarded children in state institutions. These overburdened parents seeking help through institutional care were told that there was a long waiting list.

During my administration as Governor of Minnesota, as I was pleading with the Legislature for more adequate institutional care to reduce this waiting list, I recall the anguished appeals of parents. These poor parents were up night and day for years. They often begged just for a rest, "If you can only get them into a hospital for a month or six weeks so we can get a rest," they pleaded. It was then I realized something drastic had to be done.

After discussion with Dr. Ralph Rossen, our first Mental Health Commissioner, that great humanitarian and leader in mental health whom I had the privilege of appointing, and Dr. Milton Brown, Superintendent of the Hastings Mental Hospital, a plan was devised for setting up emergency facilities for children at Hastings in a separate building which formerly housed adult mentally ill patients to take care of emergency cases of mentally retarded children on the waiting list.

In order to relieve the pressure on as many parents as possible whose retarded children were on the waiting list, the children were rotated every six weeks. But we realized this was only a stop-gap and we intensified our fight for adequate institutional facilities.

Unfortunately, there are still waiting lists. In fact, some have grown even longer through the years.

Last year I was given the task of presiding over court sessions in the United States District Court for the District of

Columbia in which hearings were held for the commitment of mentally retarded children to the institution at Laurel, Maryland. I am happy to state that today in the District of Columbia there is virtually no waiting list. Unfortunately, this cannot be said for all the states. I have visited the fine facilities Congress has provided at Laurel, and I commend our national leaders in meeting this need.

In those early days, even though a commitment was secured, in many cases it did not have too much significance for there was no program to change the status of these children. They could only sit and stare—the lostlings of society.

These institutions were frightfully overcrowded, severely understaffed, and unable to provide the activity and recreational programs designed to rehabilitate these unfortunate children. Many of the parents were frustrated. With a sense of guilt and shame, these parents kept their children out of sight.

In addition to these difficulties, there were a number of basic social prejudices which had to be overcome. The 1960 White House Conference on Children and Youth emphasized the theme of "Opportunities for children and youth to realize their full potential for a creative life in freedom and dignity." The mentally retarded were frequently placed beyond the pale of this noble democratic goal.

However, through the efforts of the Association, men and women with wisdom and compassion are beginning to accept the mentally retarded as a part of the human family and to educate him in the things he can do, so that he may be happy in himself and useful to society.

Ten years ago public interest in the mentally retarded was so slight that the 1950 White House Conference on Children and Youth provided no place on its agenda for discussion of mental retardation. But the 1960 White House Conference gave it top priority! And so the mentally retarded are forgotten children no longer.

Due principally to the vision, courage and devotion of the members of the National Association for Retarded Children, despair has been transformed into hope.

Through many hundred units in the various states, the Association has enlisted the efforts of parents and friends in behalf of the retarded. This organization has been outstanding in coordinating the activity of the local units; in serving as a clearing house for the dissemination of scientific information and in securing increased support from legislators for research and community clinics and better institutional care.

But of equal significance have been the by-products of the movement started by the Association. Of course, there is always the by-product of people discovering their capabilities when they find themselves with this kind of leadership challenge. During the past ten years we have seen everything happen to leaders: die, become ill, physically or mentally or both; we have witnessed the psychopathology of groups and the various drives for power and prestige—both among parents and professional workers; but we have seen some fantastic evidences of personal growth and productivity, and not a few professional workers have gained some well-deserved status from sincere efforts. Parents have discovered they could write, give speeches and, most important, that in merely giving of themselves and their experience, they have found true meaning in their lives and in their suffering and have created meaning for their children's existence. In other words, there are countless opportunities for ordinary people to help others which, if done with insight and know-how, can supplement and transcend the professional activities.

But possibly the greatest by-product of all is reflected in the statement of Dr. Howard A. Rusk when he said, "I believe that this basic and inherent desire of man to do something for his less fortunate fellow man transcends religious dogmas, political beliefs and geographic barriers. If we could only use this universal language, we would have a tool to unravel the Babel of tongues and an instrument which would penetrate any iron curtain or closed boundary." And of course this has happened through our international associations. Who knows what a terrific instrument for peace this may be, as we give increasing emphasis to reverence for human life?

We know now that a vast number of retarded children can be trained in basic skills and be prepared for gainful employment.

In the early years of the organization, they rightly concentrated upon better residential treatment for the 140,000 retardates in state institutions. During the past decade many of the states have built new schools for the retarded to relieve the frightful overcrowding. Although more than 10,000 beds were added to the nation's public institutions for the mentally retarded, there is still a backlog today of approximately 15,000 children awaiting admission to these institutions. In my own State of Minnesota, the appropriation of $17 million for capital construction in the field of mental retardation has still not brought us abreast of the backlog.

However, it is important to note that there have been significant improvements in the medical, educational, recreational and vocational programs offered by these institutions.

In many of the better institutions, activities running the gamut from school instruction to vocational rehabilitation and good, healthy recreational programs are the order of the day.

But much more must be done. It is deeply depressing to look at official figures from the National Institute of Mental Health which show that only about 5,000 mentally retarded children were discharged from public institutions in 1958 as against the admission that year of 13,500 retardates.

I hold a deep-seated conviction that institutionalization should be the last resort—that all of us must devote the maximum effort to maintain most of these children in the community where they can draw upon the strengths of the home, the church and the school.

Since 1950 there has been a national trend resulting in community facilities for the mentally retarded. All over the country this trend—usually with the help of vocational rehabilitation—has resulted in returning the higher grade retarded person to the community and in assisting him to secure work. These community facilities have been of many types and they have made it possible for retarded persons in greater numbers to remain in the community or return to the community from a state institution. This should be intensified in the years ahead. Because of this, however, there is a much higher percentage in institutions needing definite physical care and personal direction in their daily living than in the past.

The increase in community facilities, including public school classes, will mean that the institution will become a more specialized place for many who need a period of special observation, treatment and training in order to return to the community. It will, in many instances, continue to serve as a permanent home for those who present physical or other problems too great to be cared for in the local community, or those of lower intelligence without families to provide love and interest.

During my administration as Governor, one of the first things I did administratively, as far as the retarded program was concerned, was to eliminate an arbitrary "I.Q." below which it was considered impossible to help the child.

We inaugurated the policy that every effort should be made to help every child, regardless of how retarded he might be. This ought to be a universal policy.

Even if it is realized that some retarded children may remain in an institution all their lives, efforts should be made to teach nonambulatory patients to walk and to teach almost completely helpless patients to feed themselves, at least partially.

Of all the accomplishments the Association has brought into being during the last decade, the most notable has been the insistence upon individual diagnosis of each child and the development of a comprehensive training program tailored to that child's needs. At the recently concluded London Conference of the Scientific Study of Mental Deficiency, Dr. R. A. Jensen, Professor of Psychiatry and Pediatrics at the University of Minnesota Medical School, emphasized the importance of a careful physiological and psychological evaluation of each child.

Precise diagnosis must be tied in closely with pre-school education and training of the retarded child. The monumental study by Dr. Samuel Kirk, "Early Education of the Mentally Retarded," demonstrates beyond doubt that children who have properly directed pre-school training based on adequate diagnosis are in a much better position to benefit from public school and vocational training programs.

In 1950 there wasn't a single diagnostic clinic in the country for evaluation of the mentally retarded. It is heartening to note that today there are seventy of these clinics, most of them supported by grants from the U. S. Children's Bureau. However, these clinics have long waiting lists, and it is vitally important that the Association continue the crusade for the opening of more clinics.

Beyond the need for clinics, the Association has grasped the need for a whole host of community resources designed to bring to full development the many potentials of the retarded child. Among the most significant progressive developments in the past decade, I include the following:

1. *EDUCATION*

Spectacular progress has been made in the provisions of educational opportunities for the mentally retarded child. Forty-eight states now have legislation providing for special classes for the mentally retarded in the public schools. This compares with only twenty-four states which had such specialized programs in 1950. Furthermore, in 1950 no state had laws encouraging local districts to provide for the "trainable" mentally retarded (those with an I.Q. of 25 to 50). Today, twenty states have either mandatory or permissive legislation under which such children are provided for in the public school system.

Public school classes have been provided not only for the brighter group of the retarded—usually called educable—but also for the group called trainable. These are children who cannot be expected to enter into competitive industry, ordinarily speaking, but who can be taught not only habits in self-care and personal adjustment, but simple tasks that will make them helpful around the home, and in some instances, able to earn some money under very sheltered conditions.

While it is indeed gratifying that more than 120,000 mentally retarded children were enrolled in special classes in the public schools of our nation last year, we still have a long way to go. We are gradually overcoming the shortage of teachers of the mentally retarded. The passage in 1958 by the Congress of a 10-year authorization for the training of teachers of the mentally retarded is a magnificent step forward in this area. Furthermore, the cooperative research program of the U. S. Office of Education has, in the past few years, earmarked sizeable sums for a study of better techniques in the education of the mentally retarded. In 1950 only a few colleges and universities offered courses for preparation of teachers for the retarded. This year some 200 institutions offer such courses.

2. RELIGION

In 1950, there were practically no programs of religious instruction for the mentally retarded. Today, there are hundreds of classes through which Roman Catholic, Protestant and Jewish children are receiving religious instruction. In a further development, new day and residential schools for mentally retarded children are being organized under Roman Catholic, Lutheran, Presbyterian, Episcopalian, Jewish and other auspices.

3. RECREATION

The first summer day camp for mentally retarded children was organized in 1950. Today more than 150 such camps are in existence, and a sizeable number of residential camp programs have also been established.

Having a life-long interest in scouting, I am particularly pleased with the growth of scouting activities among the mentally retarded. Although there were Boy Scout Troops in a few residential institutions as far back as the 1920's, the first troop of retarded scouts in the community was not formed until 1950. Today more than 150 troops of mentally retarded boys are registered with the Boy Scouts of America.

4. *WELFARE*

Up until very recently, welfare agencies generally made little effort to supply the supporting services necessary to keep the mentally retarded child in the community—they were always in a hurry to get the child into an institution. I am happy to note that Minnesota has always been an outstanding exception to this; its community welfare programs for the mentally retarded date back to the early 1920's.

In recent years we have seen a quickened interest on the part of the social work profession in the problems of the mentally retarded. For example, the National Conference on Social Welfare in 1959 included four sessions dealing with the problems of the mentally retarded.

5. *VOCATIONAL REHABILITATION*

Here again spectacular gains have been recorded in the past decade. The National Association for Retarded Children deserves a major part of the credit for the fact that there are today in this country more than one hundred sheltered workshops and training centers for the mentally retarded which offer excellent job-training resources.

Even more encouraging is the fact that the National Office of Vocational Rehabilitation is currently supporting twenty-one research or demonstration projects on ways in which the mentally retarded can be rehabilitated. Recently, the office of Vocational Rehabilitation issued a report detailing how 1,100 mentally retarded young adults were able to earn more than $1,800,000 in their first year after rehabilitation.

6. STATE SERVICES

Having been the Chief Executive of a state for a number of years, I take particular pride in noting that many new and challenging state programs have been developed over the past decade to improve the lot of the mentally retarded. To cite but a few examples:

The New York State Department of Mental Hygiene has set up an office of Mental Retardation to plan and coordinate all services for the mentally retarded in that state. Illinois has established a section on Mental Retardation in its Department of Welfare, and in New Jersey the Bureau of Mental Retardation has been elevated to the status of a Division in the Department of Institutions and Agencies. Massachusetts is pioneering in the establishment of nursery centers for pre-school mentally retarded children, and currently operates twenty-seven of these centers. Delaware has a comparable program with four nursery centers in operation.

The Ohio Division of Mental Hygiene is currently supporting 220 community classes for mentally retarded youth excluded from public schools. More than half of the funds for these classes comes from the local community. Pacific State Hospital in California has established a professional training program in mental retardation. Minnesota has operated a pioneer social development center for young adult retardates too old to participate in the special school classes.

As a nation, we are spending a pitiably small amount of money on research into mental retardation. At the Federal and State level, we are spending only about $5 million for research in this field—less than three per cent of what the states spend each year for mere custody of the victims of mental retardation.

The entire field of mental illness offers a striking example of the enormous benefits resulting from a relatively small investment in research. From the time of the establishment of the first public mental hospital in Williamsburg in 1773, there was a seemingly inevitable annual rise in the number of patients housed in our state mental institutions. Working with the Governors of other states, we got the Council of State Governments to make two monumental studies of ways in which we could reduce the burden of mental illness in this nation. Both studies recommended, as a first priority, the initiation of research programs devoted to developing new methods of treatment.

You all know the dramatic results. With the advent of the tranquilizing drugs, and with the intensive participation of many of the state mental hospitals in their clinical evaluation, there has been an unprecedented reduction of 16,000 patients in our state hospitals over the past four years.

I am confident that we can achieve the same results in the field of mental retardation. The old defeatist attitude that mental deficiency could not be successfully treated has given way in the past decade to an exciting burst of research discoveries which point the way to the eventual conquest of many forms of mental retardation.

Research scientists have already identified ten metabolic disorders in the field of mental retardation, and they have developed corrective diets and other ameliorating procedures for several of these disorders. At the University of Michigan, research workers have reported the use of thyroid to prevent cretinism, one of the most common forms of mental retardation. The U. S. Public Health Service has mounted a major medical research offensive against mongolism, which afflicts more than 35,000 infants born each year. There is some evidence that mongolism may be triggered even before pregnancy, due to an irregularity in the human egg before it is fertilized.

In the increasing belief that most mental deficiency is triggered before or during pregnancy, the National Institute of Neurological Diseases and Blindness, in cooperation with medical schools and hospitals in all parts of the country, has launched a ten-year investigation of the physiological make-up of selected mothers who may give birth to normal or abnormal children. This massive project will seek to evaluate such facts as heredity, lack of oxygen, brain injuries, blood incompatibility, and infections during pregnancy in the causation of various types of mental retardation.

Testifying earlier this year before a Congressional Committee, the Association's distinguished president, Dr. Elizabeth Boggs, summarized this new era of hope in the following words:

"In 1950, when the National Association for Retarded Children was founded in Minneapolis, the field of mental retardation presented a dismal picture not only because of the inadequacies of facilities and the negative attitudes of the public and of educational, clinical, and social service agencies toward work with this group of handicapped people, but there was also an almost total lack of research activity. Today, ten years later, the picture has undergone a change so revolutionary as to be almost inconceivable. Not only are some of the finest minds in some of our most distinguished universities at work to investigate mental retardation and its causes—we actually have achieved in this short span of time, success in instituting at least the beginnings of definite preventive programs.

"To be precise, today successful scientific research has presented us with diagnostic tools and therapeutic procedures to prevent mental retardation in children who five years ago would have been so damaged as to require lifelong institutionalization."

The states are beginning to move forward in the field of research on mental retardation. Illinois is constructing a new pediatric institute devoted to training and research in the field of mental retardation; New York has expanded its research in the field of mental retardation; New York has expanded its research programs at Letchworth Village, Willowbrook and Creedmoor, and California is developing the Pacific State School into one of the finest research installations in the country.

In 1958, the Council of State Governments held a special conference on mental retardation which emphasized, as its key recommendation, that "Every State appropriate funds for research in the field of mental retardation and that these funds should be made available on a continuing basis."

In implementing this recommendation, I urge you to speak forcefully to your State Governors and your State Legislators as to the absolute necessity for research appropriations of sizeable amount in the field of mental retardation.

As we rejoice in the advances of the past decade, we must not become smug or complacent. Eternal vigilance is not only the price of liberty, but also the price that must be paid if the retarded children are to be kept out of the class of the lostlings of society.

Officials should be constantly alerted to their responsibility of vigorous leadership in behalf of these children.

There are still long waiting lists of retarded children needing institutionalization. Many of our institutions are still dangerously overcrowded, and unless research is hastened, millions of dollars must go into more institutions for children whose care must be paid for by public funds. How much wiser it would be to pay for scientific research which would make such care unnecessary.

Many of the children now mentally retarded need not have been so. More than half now mentally retarded can, with proper education, live and work in normal society.

In an article which appeared in a 1950 issue of the *Ladies' Home Journal* (and condensed in the September, 1950 issue of the *Reader's Digest*) Pearl S. Buck pours out her heart as she describes her own experiences with her retarded child. It has both incalculable comfort to parents facing a similar problem and an inspiration to anyone who has ever encountered such a sorrow.

Said Mrs. Buck, "There must be acceptance, the knowledge that sorrow fully accepted brings its own gifts. For there is an alchemy in sorrow. It can be transmuted into wisdom which can bring happiness."

May I share with you the creed of the disabled patients at the famous Institute for Physical Medicine and Rehabilitation in New York City. May it serve as an inspiration to you as you battle in the years to come to achieve a full and productive life for the mentally retarded of this nation.

I asked God for strength, that I might achieve
I was made weak, that I might learn humbly to obey . . .

I asked for health, that I might do greater things
I was given infirmity, that I might do better things . . .

I asked for riches, that I might be happy
I was given poverty, that I might be wise . . .

I asked for power, that I might have the praise of men
I was given weakness, that I might feel the need of
God . . .

I asked for all things, that I might enjoy life
I was given life, that I might enjoy all things . . .

I got nothing that I asked for—but everything I had
hoped for

Almost despite myself, my unspoken prayers were
answered
I am among all men, most richly blessed!

Edwin Markham has stated:

"There is a destiny that makes us brothers,
None goes his way alone.
All that we put into the lives of others,
Comes back into our own."

We plead with the people of our nation to do justice to our sick children in the name of Him who said "Inasmuch as ye have done it unto the least of these, my brethren, ye have done it unto me."

CHAPTER VIII

Making Your Life Count

I should like to discuss with you three essentials for making your life count for a better world.

The first essential is to realize that each individual can make something out of his life if he will understand that education is for all of life. Without in any way attempting to minimize or disparage the achievement of graduates of our schools and colleges, we should not overlook the fact that there is a difference between graduation and education.

A young lady said to her physician just prior to her operation, "How soon will I know anything, Doctor, after I come out of the anesthetic?" "Well, young lady," replied the doctor, "that is expecting a great deal from the anesthetic!" Likewise, it is expecting a great deal from the high school training to assume that one is fully equipped for the problems of life upon graduation.

Matthew Arnold, the great English educator, has said that "culture is the disinterested endeavor for perfection; the eternal becoming something finer, better and more useful in life; an endeavor which never ceases; an endeavor which loses all of its power if it ceases for a moment to become disinterested, and which loses all its beauty if it is for less an ideal than that of perfection."

Education, in its restricted sense, means training in educational institutions; in its broadest sense, means the development of all the powers of man; in its restricted application it is confined to school age; in its broadest sense it begins at the cradle and ends at the grave.

Ever since man came upon the earth there has been a constant struggle to overcome his environment, and the progress from savagery to the present stage of civilization of the most enlightened people is the result of this struggle.

We pride ourselves on the marvelous achievements of our age, but as we stand on the threshold of the space age, is there anyone so foolhardy as to suggest we have learned all there is to know?

> *"There's no sense in going further,*
> *'Tis the end of civilization,*
> *So they said and I believed it,*
> *'Till a voice as loud as thunder*
> *Rang interminable changes on one*
> *   everlasting whisper,*
> *Day and night repeated,*
> *Something hidden, go and find it,*
> *Go and look behind the ranges,*
> *Something lost behind the ranges,*
> *Lost and waiting for you. Go!"*

In the past one hundred years we have discovered many wonderful things. We have learned to harness steam and cause it to do much of our heavy labor; we have laid hold of that mysterious and mystical force known as electricity and it has been compelled to reveal many of its secrets. By and through it we talk to far-distant friends and reach out into space and bring into our homes the strains of beautiful music and the voices of those hundreds of miles away. We have perfected the internal combustion engine and by its use we speed over ribbons of concrete and when we are dissatisfied with that mode of travel, we take to the wings of morning and soar into the air.

One hundred years ago man used candles of tallow and wax for light. Now he uses the power that flashes from the lightning. A number of years ago the illumination of hundreds of millions of candle power lighting the exposition at Chicago started with the light of the distant star—Arcturus —light that had been travelling through space for forty years at the speed of 186 thousand miles per second.

Despite these advancements, great frontiers are still ahead if we will but look behind the ranges. Today ten million people are employed directly or indirectly in industries which scarcely existed at the turn of the century—motion pictures, radio, television, automobile, air-conditioning, aeronautics and electronics. The probable erection within the next few decades of millions of new homes in the United States will present a problem on which trained young minds might well concentrate.

There is an acute shortage of skilled men in various industries. New opportunities in agriculture appear on every hand. Social service work is finding a permanently enlarged sphere in American life. Then the space age presents an entirely new frontier.

Some say there are too many people these days getting an education. This is not a fact. There may be too many people going to school, but you can't give too many people an education.

In view of the many encouraging developments in adult education, there are more people than ever engaged in the disinterested endeavor to become better educated.

It is a pathetic and unnecessary fact that many people do not learn anything after they are twenty-five years of age, and many of them learn nothing after they are 15 or 20! This is not because they cannot learn, but because they have never learned how to learn anything new. They have minds that are good enough, but no use for them. Except for carrying them through their daily routine of doing their house work or office work, or attending committee meetings, organizations for keeping things as they are, or making money, their minds are of no more use to them or anyone else.

For a long time it was claimed by many that man had reached his climax at 40 and from then on is on the downhill road and that he should be chloroformed at 60. Experiments all indicate that a man has reached the deadline when he ceases to learn. Some reach this at 20, others at 40, still others at 60, while some never reach it at all. You have reached the deadline when you display your diploma or your union card or your stenographer's or accountant's certificate and say, "I have finished my education." That is the day you have really chloroformed yourself and are mentally dead.

Some years ago the lives of 400 of the world's greatest men and women were investigated and it was found that the greatest achievements were at the average age of 50 and that some of them had done their greatest work at the age of 70 and some even at 80 years of age! We die mentally the day we cease our efforts to learn.

There is a fine saying attributed to Michelangelo that expresses the central maxim of this whole psychology of education. Michelangelo was made superintending architect of St. Peter's Cathedral on his seventy-second birthday and he carried on through the reign of five Popes. When he was nearly ninety and had lost his eyesight and had become enfeebled in body, he still had his servants carry him into the great temple. As he ran those marvelous hands of his—marvelous because he had kept on using them—over the statues and decorations, the old blind man exclaimed, "I still learn, I still learn."

Whether you have a great mind or a common mind; whether you are a genius or just an average man or woman, you are still a vital factor in your home, your workshop, your community and the world as long as you can say with old, blind Michelangelo, "I still learn."

There is a great frontier before each one of you, no matter what may be your calling. The individual with the average I.Q.—the so-called ordinary common man, is much under-rated. The common man may be the mailman, the operator of a streetcar, the one who waits on you at the store, or who works at the next desk in your office. He holds the key to many situations. It is all very well to be impressed by the contributions to human happiness by the world's leaders— the great men and women who do things and do them well, and who usually get the publicity, the praise and the rewards. But we sometimes forget that behind them are unnumbered hosts of ordinary men and women whose names are never emblazoned in the eight-column streamers of the press; whose faces are never captured by the news-reel cameras; but whose quiet, devoted and consecrated and unassuming work makes the task of leaders possible.

Dr. Paul Rees has said, "If history teaches anything, it tells us that God seems to have a fondness for getting hold of very commonplace persons and transferring them into uncommon saints, or leaders, or reformers, or preachers, or missionaries. Where did He get Moses? Out of the obscurity of an humble home among the Hebrew slaves in Egypt. Where did He get Gideon? Out of the obscurity of a little wheat farm in Ephraim. Where did He get David? Out of the obscurity of the large family of Jesse where fame had never been known to rest. Where did He get Peter and John? Out of the obscurity of their unheralded toil as fishermen. Where did He get Dwight L. Moody? Out of the obscurity of a little shoe store lost among the big palaces of merchandise in Boston.

"These tales are endless in God's great pattern of doing things. They call us to sound thinking. They summon us to clear judgments of value. They tell us that obscurity should never stifle or strangle us. They drive home the truth that, however undistinguished persons we may be, we can serve our God in a distinguished way."

The vast majority of people fall into the class of the average men and women who are always taken for granted, but without whom nothing could be accomplished. They have a job to do and they do it willingly and without grumbling or complaining and often with bravery and consecration of the highest order. They are willing not only to lose their identities in the job to be done, but even to lose their lives for the sake of others. Edgar Guest puts it this way:

> *"The backbone of the nation*
> *Is the happy-hearted throng*
> *Of ordinary people*
> *Who go swinging right along.*
>
> *They live in modest houses*
> *And they work from day to day.*

And the papers never notice
What they do or what they say!"

You no doubt have read of the retreat to Dunkirk in World War II after the collapse of the Maginot Line and the surrender of Belgium. Covering the retreat was the 51st Division of the British Army. They stood at St. Valerie to make evacuation possible. They were a road-block whose only job was to hold back the Panzer Division long enough to permit the motley fleet of small boats to take off as many British and French soldiers as possible. They were lost. *Expendable*. But they made Dunkirk possible. They were common soldiers, but they stood between the forces of slavery and freedom. It does not take the great men to accomplish great things.

J. C. Penny said, "If I could get a message over to the young people of the country, indeed—of the world—it would be: to succeed in life does not require genius. No boy ever worried more about his future and making a success, or ever left his home town with prospects visibly less bright than I. Certainly genius was *not* one of my qualities. Any young man or woman of ordinary intelligence who is morally sound, open and above-board in human dealings, not afraid of work, prepared to play the game fairly and squarely and keep everlastingly at it can succeed in spite of handicaps and obstacles!"

Years before he was President, Abraham Lincoln, while on a visit to New York City, was asked one Sunday morning to make some remarks to a Sunday School class in an industrial institution. The children gathered there came from an environment of penury, the parents of most of them having been born in Europe. A listener took down what Lincoln said that day to the Sunday School group. He spoke on what it meant to be an American. Here are two sentences: "You children must always thank God that you have been born in a country where, if you will lead a decent, clean life, trust God, work hard, you can rise. The only things that will limit you are your industry, your character, and your brains." He was telling those so-called underprivileged youngsters that because they were in America the way was open to the top.

"I bargained with life for a penny;
And found that life would give me no more;
No matter how much I begged at evening,
When I counted my scanty store.

I bargained with life for a penny,
Only to find, dismayed,
No matter what wage I had asked of Life,
Life would have paid!"

The second characteristic required to make your life count is that of courage.

The records of every educational institution show hundreds of cases of young people who are battling under a lowered physical vitality; often with actual disease, tuberculosis, diabetes, anemia, and similar disorders. One university records an honor student who spent half of the four years in a plaster cast due to an inherited physical condition. Another who has kept alive by the daily use of insulin. Another with a collapsed lung; a fourth who, on the eve of graduation, was ordered to a tubercular sanitarium. These youngsters have taken it on the chin and won honors and faced the future with undaunted hopefulness and heroic spirit.

History records the greatness of countless people who accepted the challenge of their handicaps and outdid those normally endowed. Demosthenes, the greatest orator of ancient Greece, overcame speech impediments by orating to the waves with his mouth full of pebbles, and declaiming as he ran up hill. John Milton dictated "Paradise Lost" after he had gone blind. Beethoven, when deaf, penned some of his finest music. Auguste Renoir, doubled up with paralysis, had brushes strapped to his hands so he could paint pictures. Steinmetz, the electrical genius, was a hunchback and cripple.

Down in Kansas a number of years ago, two young boys entered a country schoolhouse. They lighted an old kerosene stove and it exploded, causing the whole building to go up in flames. One of the brothers rushed out safely, but upon discovering that his brother was still inside, he retraced his steps, ran in amidst the flames to find only a charred body. He was critically burned. The doctor was called and found the flesh falling off the victim. The words the boy heard the doctor say that day were, "He will never walk again." Several years passed. At the age of 11, he was hobbling around on crutches. The boys of the neighborhood would sneer at him and say, "He can't run like we do." But this young lad had determination. He had decided to conquer the challenge the doctor had made several years back. At 13, he had discarded the crutches and would secretly go after his father's cows on the farm. As a junior at the Kansas High School, he won the letter in track. He enrolled in the University of Kansas and made a mark for himelf in his running achievements and today the name of Glenn Cunningham stands foremost among the world's greatest milers.

The most stimulating successes in history have come from persons who, facing some kind of limitation and handicap, refuse to take it as some part of life's fate and have gone on to noble achievement.

The third characteristic required to make your life count is that of character. We need more than intellectual literacy —more especially do we need social, moral and spiritual literacy.

The great frontier before every individual in this space age is in the realm of the spirit. It was distressing to read recently a dispatch relating to a New York City junior high school. A fine arts teacher had a class of high quality with intelligence quotients of 130 and above. The teacher asked them what they would wish for more than anything else in the world. Thirty-seven out of thirty-nine named the acquisition of money as the main aim of their lives. That is disconcerting when one considers the tremendously challenging frontiers before the graduates today in the realm of the spirit. Every individual is a part of the ideological struggle between godless communism and our way of life. We cannot hope to win in the economic, military or political fields alone. Our victory must be won in the realm of the spirit.

As someone has said, "to be an American is to believe, as we look at any man, that he is a child of God—no matter what the color of his skin, the accident of his birth, or the particular creed which he may profess. America is not a thing of the earth, but a thing of the heart. It is a way of thinking and a way of acting. It is not bounded by oceans, rivers or degrees of latitude, but by principles, attitudes and ideals more precious than life itself. America is a classless society whose aristocracy is based not on pedestals but on personalities; not on birth but on worth; not on who you are, but on what you are."

John D. Rockefeller, Jr. has given us, I think, a beautiful creed to which every high school graduate should subscribe: "I believe in the supreme worth of the individual and in his right to life, liberty and the pursuit of happiness. I believe that every right implies a responsibility; an obligation; and every possession, a duty. I believe that the law was made for man and not man for the law; that government is the servant of the people, and not their master. I believe in the dignity of labor, whether with head or hand; that the world owes no man a living, but that it owes every man an opportunity to make a living. I believe that thrift is essential to well-ordered living and that economy is a prime requisite of a sound financial structure—whether in government, business or personal affairs. I believe that truth and justice are fundamental to an enduring social order. I believe in the sacredness of a promise, that a man's word should be as good as his bond; that character—not wealth or power or position—is of useful service to mankind and that only in the purifying fire of sacrifice is the dross of selfishness consumed and the greatness of the human soul set free. I believe in an all-wise and all-loving God, named by whatever name, and that the individual's highest fulfillment, greatest happiness and widest usefulness are to be found in living in harmony with His will. I believe that love is the greatest thing in the world; that it alone can overcome hate; that right can and will triumph over might!"

Strong character is our greatest bastion of freedom. Dr. Arnold Lowe has said: "A man in politics without character is a festering sore and a source of corruption. A statesman without character is a threat to peace and security. He can ruin us. A business man without character is an exploiter of the skill of those who work with him. An educator without character is a purloiner of mere facts and falsehoods. A jurist without character sells his power for favoritism. A minister without character is a false prophet and a seducer of the minds of men. Married people without character are selfish creatures who sacrifice their children for the sake of personal gratification." And I might add that a nation without character in this space age is doomed. Our cause is lost unless we move forward as a nation under God.

One of the great stories of heroism in World War II illustrates the ideals that we must follow in finding our destiny. It is the story of Lt. Col. John Henry Patterson, a citizen soldier killed in the service of his country. His body lies on the summit of Mount Oliveto in the Apennine Mountains of Italy. His character and deeds ought to inspire us to better and nobler living in a world of peace.

Patterson had been superintendent of schools in Phoenix, Arizona. The qualities which made him a good teacher made him also a good leader of men. Between the time he landed on Salerno Beach and his untimely death on October 2, 1943, he had carried out seven difficult missions with the phenomenally low casualty list of seven men out of the entire battalion.

According to the story coming out of the war, Oliveto was Patterson's last important mission. It is a dominating hill from which the Germans were interdicting the road to Ponte di Benevento. There was no advancing until that height was taken, and a combined operation with Col. Patterson's battalion, supported by tanks and artillery, was planned.

The artillery did its stuff, but when the tanks went in they found that the enemy's observation from that height was so accurate that it would have been suicidal to go on. The Germans had a battery of 88's up there, machine gun nests and infantry clustered around a sort of saddle in the hill.

Col. Patterson would have been justified in holding back until a larger force could be assembled for the operation, but he had never failed to carry out a mission before and certainly he had never turned back.

He went out with a patrol and studied the terrain. There were two gullies that climbed on each side of Oliveto to the heights above that saddle where the Germans were concentrated. If the gullies could be reached it would not be the Nazis, but the Americans who commanded the higher positions and the issue could not long remain in doubt after that.

And so Oliveto was taken—a feint at the center while under the cover of darkness the main force climbed those gullies to high points, then swung down to take the Germans on both flanks. It was such a surprise that they captured those three precious 88's before the enemy could even spike them.

Not a single American soldier was killed or wounded, so the total now was eight missions, seven casualties. Ponte di Benevento was taken and the regiment moved north.

The march to victory, however, was not to be completed by Patterson. An orderly walking in his rear tripped over a wire, exploding a mine which killed Patterson and wounded two non-coms. Patterson, thus, is one of the nearly 400,000 Americans who gave their lives between 1941 and 1945 that the rest of us might continue to live in peace and freedom.

Shortly before his death, Patterson, out of his experience in mountain warfare, suggested a text for a sermon to his best friend, the regimental chaplain: "Always take the high ground and the enemy will flee."

The chaplain used that text at the burial service for the man who took Mount Oliveto. It is a good text for those who strive in the battles of peace to achieve a political and social order at home and abroad worthy of the sacrifices of Patterson and the other fallen heroes.

> *"To every man there openeth a way and ways*
>   *and a way,*
> *A high soul climbs the high way,*
> *And the low soul gropes the low;*
> *And in between, on the misty flats,*
> *The rest drift to and fro.*
> *To every man there openeth*
> *A high way and a low,*
> *And every man decideth*
> *The way his soul shall go."*

CHAPTER IX

Political Penicillin

It is an inspiration to be present on this memorable occasion which brings together representatives of Zonta International, the forward-looking organization of executive and professional women.

In choosing the theme for the convention, "Tomorrow's future—Today," evidence was given of the realization that what the individual does today determines what tomorrow is to be like. The inexorable fact is recognized that if we are to have a decent future we must dedicate our lives today. The record of services by Zonta International in working for children, for the handicapped, for human welfare, indicates a sincere effort to help in this noble cause.

Your organization convened to consider the key role women must take today for leadership and influence at an hour when the free world is in the throes of crisis. It is a crisis that has its most violent manifestation in the flaming villages and raging battles of Korea and arises out of a sharp ideological conflict. It is a conflict pertaining to the nature of truth and the nature of the individual. The cardinal democratic concept, holding that the individual is the most precious thing on earth, is at stake in this conflict.

The word for "crisis" in the Chinese language results from combining two characters, one meaning "opportunity," the other "danger."

So the word "crisis," in describing the age in which we live, serves to remind us that it is a time of great opportunity, as well as danger—if we are equal to the challenge of events.

We shall be able to overcome the danger and utilize the opportunity only if we are willing to pay the price for freedom by individual discipline and consecration.

A great English historian, Lord Macaulay, gave us due warning as to the nature of the greatest threat to our survival. Back in 1852, in writing about America he said, "Either some Caesar or Napoleon will seize the reins of government with a strong hand; or your republic will be as savagely plundered and laid waste by barbarians in the 20th Century as the Roman Empire was in the 5th—with this difference— that the Huns and vandals who ravaged the Roman Empire came from without, and that your Huns and vandals will have been engendered within your own country by your own institutions."

In the light of recent findings by Senate Investigating Committees and other warning signs, it is clear that we need to be ever alert to avoid the fate Lord Macaulay predicted for us. Though Lord Macaulay was berated for his remarks as to America a century ago, who can honestly deny them now? Who can deny that our Huns and vandals are today the product of our own individual apathy?

Now, as always, the essential ingredient in effective, vital democracy is one thing alone — individual willingness to shoulder responsibility for the conduct of government. Lose that, and we are doomed to crumble and deteriorate from

within. The saving of our way of life from destruction is not
a job delegated solely to a group of young men fighting and
dying on the hills and in the valleys of Korea. It is a job delegated to every citizen. Whether we shall survive the inner
dangers hinges on whether we are willing to recognize the
individual responsibility that is ours.

The inner threats are moral threats, weaknesses of national character. They can be overcome; they must be overcome. Members of Zonta International in America and in all
free nations have a special responsibility in overcoming the
over-shadowing threat. For Zonta International is composed
of women who have, by their achievements, earned themselves
a place of recognition and leadership in many walks of life.
By standards of success, they have attained high places. And
because they have attained high places, they have an opportunity to do more, to give exceptional leadership in the fight
to strengthen our nation from within. They must be "executives of democracy." Because of exceptional abilities, they
have an unusual opportunity to inspire and guide more
women into political affairs at all levels of government. This
is direly needed. The moral force of women has always been
a wholesome influence. We have a great need for much more
of that influence.

I think that Clare Luce has aptly pointed to the need as
follows: "Faced with most contemporary questions, modern
man has been too prone to ask 'is it good for business, or
good for the profit system? Is it good for my labor union or
my political party?' Woman asks, rather, 'Is it good for the
family, the children?' For woman knows what man has too
long forgotten—that the ultimate economic and spiritual
unit of any civilization is still the family, and that all questions should be answered with respect to the well-being, hap-

piness and solidarity of the individual family unit."

Women, because of their special interests in life, are naturally concerned more about human values than about material values; more about people than dollars. So their interests lean towards the welfare of schools and the care of the neglected child, the handicapped, the aged. This foremost concern in human values is the quality of character essential in sustaining and strengthening our way of life.

America's future is being determined today. It is decided by our day-by-day acceptance of responsibilities in the building of character in youth and in the preserving of human resources.

Members of Zonta International, in accepting a special responsibility of leadership that is theirs, by virtue of proven skill and prominence in other careers, should give their best in showing the people of the home community that the individual citizen does have power to help shape the course of democracy. This is sometimes, unfortunately, difficult for the average citizen to appreciate.

So often we hear a person say, "Well, what can I do about this or that? I am just a poor insignificant mortal. I haven't any influence. This matter of building a better world is such a stupendous thing, it is out beyond my reach." This attitude is reflected in the findings of Murray G. Ross, a prominent social scientist, who recently conducted a survey among a representative cross-section of 2,000 young people between the ages of 18 to 29. One of his findings as to their attitudes was the fact that they do not consider their lives able to count for much in the larger scheme of things. This attitude of futility we must fight to overcome. It imperils the future that we want for ourselves and our children. During World War II, over 100,000 citizens jammed into the Los Angeles

Coliseum one starless night for a patriotic meeting. Suddenly, the Chairman startled the throng by saying, "Don't be afraid now—all the lights are going out." In complete darkness he struck a match. "All who can see this little light, say 'yes.' " A deafening roar came from the audience. He said, "So shines a good deed in a stricken world. But suppose now everyone of us here strikes a light." Faster than it takes to tell, nearly 100,000 pin pricks of flame flooded the entire arena with light—the result of 100,000 individuals, each doing his part. This demonstration served to aptly illustrate the part individuals can play by working together for a common cause.

We need to remember the influence of the individual as stressed in these words: "I am only one, but I am one. I can't do much, but I can do something. What I can do I ought to do, and what I ought to do, by the Grace of God, I will do!"

Few things indicate the power of one person as a general election does. Yet, in America, despite our much-vaunted educational system, we fail to make use of this power of the individual. The record of citizen participation is one that grows poorer with the passing of the years instead of brighter. In 1896, 83 per cent of the potential American voters cast their ballots at a presidential election. This percentage has been steadily dropping until in 1948, less than 50 per cent of the eligible Americans took part in the presidential election, and in 1950, when there was no presidential election, only 41 per cent of our qualified citizens utilized the power they possess in the ballot.

Do we fully realize the dangers inherent in such a trend? We need only to turn back the pages of history to find example after example of what happens when people fail to be articulate and to use their rights. Those rights simply wither and die away. For instance, there was Germany. In 1932, in the last general election before Hitler's ascent to power, just three million Germans out of sixty-five million exercised the right of the ballot. Out of that three million came the votes to put Hitler into power. It is a fairy tale to say that Hitler ascended into power by bloodshed or revolution. He ascended into power by one individual multiplied by three million. He ascended into power because many other millions were indifferent and declined to use the power that was theirs.

Someone has aptly pointed out that less than one per cent of humanity has caused most of humanity's problems. One man in Germany, one man in Italy, were instrumental in bringing about the holocaust of World War II. Today, the troubles of the present moment are brought about by one nation. This nation is controlled by a political clique composed of less than 14 men, ruled by the powerful persuasion of one man. Our job is to get one per cent and more of humanity working as consistently for a better world as another one per cent seek its destruction. If we can do this, we can well change the course of human events for the better.

In East Germany, behind the iron curtain, an 18-year-old Bavarian youth, Hermann Flade, has shown to the world one more example of the power of one individual. Whether he is still alive, I do not know. His "crime" was the distribution of leaflets calling upon the people to vote against the Communist-controlled front ticket in a Fall dummy election in Germany. He was tried and convicted as an "enemy of the State." Such trials and subsequent death penalties are no rarity behind the iron curtain. Thousands of unsung heroes have chosen death rather than to submit to ruthless rulers. They, like Hermann Flade, are the modern Patrick Henrys who choose liberty or death, and from the Kremlin they get death. In so doing, they set an example that should inspire all freedom-loving people to make good use of the rights which others have lost.

I urge you, as executives of democracy, to give your foremost efforts to leadership at the local level of government. The decline of citizen interest there is most pronounced and most dangerous.

A study of local government was made several years ago by the Council of Inter-Government Relations in one county. One of its most significant findings was this: "Local issues no longer command the attention they deserve; local elections are won and lost on the votes of a pitifully small percentage of the electorate; public attendance at meetings of government bodies is rare except when extremely controversial issues are at stake; national issues are fought in the abstract, as they affect the political or emotional leanings of the citizenry. The energies of the local people are dissipated in broadcast criticism of national action programs, rather than spent in constructive attempts to improve their administration locally—largely because these national programs have not been established or accepted generally as community ventures." Isn't that a typical appraisal of local government? In the minds of the people, government has become "they" instead of, as it should be, "we."

In some elections for city officials in our country, as few as three per cent of the registered voters will take the trouble to go to the polls.

There is a disease known as "presbyopia," in which objects very near the eye cannot be seen. Perhaps that is part of our trouble in civic affairs. Too many are like the young

man who suffered serious eye trouble and was given the following diagnosis by an oculist: "You are living on the Western prairies, where you look out constantly on a vast ex-
panse; you need something close at hand to lean your eyes
against." So, today we look over a world of turmoil. We look
at national issues. Never has the range of man's ordinary
vision taken in such a wide scope and dwelt on such immense
affairs. Many of us, too, are having trouble with our vision.
We need something close at hand to lean our eyes against.
We can find it in giving leadership and service in our own
communities.

Nothing has done more to emphasize the job that must
be done in the local community than the testimony and findings of the Senate Crime Investigating Committee. If it
brought out one thing, it brought out this—that local government is too often a weak link in the American political
system. The Committee showed the American public how effectively organized crime has been developed in our country,
how it extends across state lines and entrenches itself through
corruption of local officials. It revealed that the life blood of
the underworld is organized gambling, yielding 20 billion
dollars every year, and that the privilege of carrying on this
lucrative racket is often bought from officials who can be cor-
rupted.

The findings of the Kefauver Committee unfolded a sor-
did picture of an inner threat in our country, while providing
entertainment for millions of television viewers. When it was
all over, the Kefauver Committee gave the American people
a set of recommendations. Some of them called for changes
and additions in Federal laws. But the Committee realized
that, most important of all, the racketeers can be put out of
business only by beginning at the grass roots; that it is up to

local government to effectively wipe out this threat. Its conclusions brought us to the time-tested formula for good government—if people want good government, they can have it, whether it is at city, county, or state level. In short, it was proved once again that the people get just as bad government as they will stand for, and just as good government as they will fight for.

The Federal Government may help implement the community will, but it certainly cannot create that will. Only the people in the local community can effectively carry out the long-time, day-by-day job of correcting the conditions out of which bad government grows.

I urge that you give your attention and efforts first to the matters of local government. There, you can do the best job of helping to repair and strengthen the very foundations of democracy.

Remember that the successful functioning of our form of government is based on the premise that a majority of the people, acting on the basis of informed understanding of candidates and issues, will make wise decisions for the welfare of all the people. If only a small percentage of the voters trouble themselves to participate in the local elections, in which the candidates and issues are best known because they are close to the people, what hope then is there for wise decisions on national questions?

The future is being determined now—here in our own community. In the real battle for democracy, the home front is right in the home town. If we can't keep democracy alive and alert at home, what hope is there for making it work at the national or world level? The local community is the laboratory where we must work out the formula by which to solve the larger issues of the day. There, we should be developing the civic competence needed to qualify us for membership in the larger communities of the state, nation and the world.

Our need is for getting an aroused leadership to ring doorbells, make telephone calls, sell people on the importance of voting for good candidates and for reform. We should have a great national revival for the strengthening of local government, of awakening interest in local government. Where progress has been made in municipal reform women have invariably had a key role in bringing it to reality. The League of Women Voters and other groups of organized women are always in the forefront of the fight to clean up and modernize local government.

There are scores of examples in every part of the country of what they can accomplish. I know too that at the state level, Minnesota could not have made the progress it has achieved in good government without the constant work of women's organizations. They have been able champions for our Youth Conservation program, better care of the mentally ill, the aged, the handicapped. They have given strong leadership to the fight for better schools and for revision of our antiquated state constitution and for other worthy measures.

It is also heartening to note that women are also coming to the front as candidates in Minnesota. That is a healthy thing for the state.

It was my privilege to appoint the first woman ever to be a Judge of the Municipal Court of Minnesota. Later she won a resounding victory by a vote which topped that of all candidates. Furthermore, six out of seven women candidates won election to the Minneapolis School Board and five of them led the ticket. Two women served in our State Legislature in contrast to previous sessions which had no women as members. We have a woman giving outstanding service on our very important Youth Conservation Commission. Our state can also be proud because it has provided one of America's most able and popular ambassadors — Mrs. Eugenie Anderson.

Truly, women are demonstrating what they can do in politics. Outnumbering men as they now do, women have the opportunity to multiply these examples of success and to bring good government to all areas.

Members of Zonta International should recognize that it is not enough to be a good lawyer, or doctor, or business woman in these times of crisis. They are needed for a double role of career plus *politics*.

Someone may accuse me of being too elementary if I plead with executive and professional people to exercise the simple duty of voting. But I do know this—a survey made among a group of top business executives after the last national election showed that a deplorably small percentage of these men had voted; that, as a matter of fact, twelve per cent of them had not even registered. Perhaps a similar survey among a group of women executives would give better results. I do not know. What do you think?

We have benefited from women in party politics at the local level, but we need many more. All ought to be members of a political party. Everyone ought to be a regular attendant at his local political party caucus. How many have ever been at such a caucus? There is where you have an opportunity to choose the delegates who will shape the policies of your political party.

One Minnesota citizen who now is a faithful participant in his party's caucus tells this significant story of why he is not a stay-at-home any longer. He says of his first visit to such a meeting: "There were thirteen of us there—thirteen out of a total of over 3,000 who were able to attend. That meant seven of us controlled the meeting; that those seven could elect the delegates and decide what our party policies should be. I decided then and there that I would rather be one of the seven than one of the thousands."

Be "one of the seven"—help, through your leadership, to arouse your fellow citizens to a realization that democracy is losing ground because of their failure to participate in local government and local political parties.

Welcome the opportunity to be a candidate for public office. Be proud to be known as a politician as was Lincoln. Politics is not to be scorned; it is the art of making government work. More women are getting into the political arena, but many more are needed. If there were proportionately as many women in our U. S. Congress as there are in the Indian Parliament, we would have 85 women in Congress. Instead, we have only seven.

Be willing to stand up and be counted on political issues in the local community. Don't be guilty of letting a fear that your business may be hurt by being articulate prevent you from speaking out. Do not permit yourself to stifle a cause by saying, "I feel as strongly as you do, but in my position I can't say anything." I get letters making a plea like that— because it might hurt business—afraid to denounce graft because of fear of the retaliation by the grafters on business profits. Our need is for courageous men and women in the local community if we are to be assured of honest government serving the best interests of all the people.

Many people seem to be looking for a miracle or a panacea which will shape a future of peace and brotherhood. That is wishful thinking, a futile hope.

The only real hope lies in the day-by-day acceptance of responsibility by the individual citizen, in the building of character, in the preservation of moral values in the community with its homes and schools and churches and government.

My challenge to the women of Zonta International, leaders in many walks of life, is, if you have not already done so, to give yourselves now to a second career—a career of service and leadership in your home community. There is where America's future is being shaped and forged.

There is where you can best help bring the dawn of a new day with the future which we desire.

CHAPTER X

The Greatest of These Is Charity

I believe in the voluntary welfare agency as a vital force in American life. It is an outstanding example of our Christian religion put into practice in accordance with the essence of the teaching of Christ.

"And now abideth faith, hope, charity, these three; but the greatest of these is charity"—that is the philosophy that must be understood and followed by all who accept Christianity as a way of life.

True charity is the expression of human compassion. Without it, our churches would crumble and with them would go the last remnants of our faith and spiritual resources.

Christ taught His people that "it is more blessed to give than to receive." He emphasized the values derived from personalized giving—the type of giving that is made possible through the voluntary agencies in our nation. Christ set forth the basis of the voluntary agency when He spoke to the lawyer who came to Him for advice. This man was confused and upset by life. He was wealthy and successful, but still he was terribly unhappy, and so he begged the Teacher, who counseled His followers to "love thy neighbor," to give him the secret of inner peace.

The answer came in the form of a parable, as you will recall. Christ told about the man who was waylaid by robbers and left beaten and bruised along the road to Jericho. Two travelers had passed him by, unheeding his plight. They had their own affairs to attend to. They were in a great hurry. Finally, a third came upon the scene, a Samaritan. He, too, was a busy man and bound for other places. But seeing the distress of a fellow man, bound up his wounds, carried him to an inn, and arranged for his care.

Jesus then said, "Which now of these three, thinkest thou, was neighbor unto him that fell among thieves?" And he said, "He that showed mercy on him." Then said Jesus unto him, "Go, and do thou likewise."

The parable of the good Samaritan charts the way for fruitful Christian living. Millions of Americans become "good Samaritans" by the opportunities provided them to give and serve in the voluntary welfare agencies of the churches of all faiths.

Our world witnesses a death struggle between the philosophies of Christ and Karl Marx. If the triumph of Christ is to come, it will be only by our putting into practice a renewed spirit of compassion as "good Samaritans." It can best be generated by voluntary welfare agencies and by individual devotion to service to one's fellow men.

And so, in this struggle of diverse ideologies, we need the voluntary welfare agency more than ever before. We must depend upon it to establish the standards for government agencies that are also in the welfare field and spur them forward. We must continue to look to the leadership of the voluntary organization to create and sustain the system of morals upon which our free society is founded.

The National Conference of Catholic Charities has, I know, carried on a gallant fight to maintain and strengthen the role of the voluntary agency in national life. Monsignor O'Grady, as Secretary of the Conference, has been an able spokesman in this relentless effort to preserve one of the finest and most fundamental institutions of American life. In acknowledging this outstanding service, as carried on by Catholic Charities, we are well aware that in many countries the first attacks on the Church have been aimed at its charities. All religious faiths, therefore, must join in this effort to preserve voluntary charity work of the churches.

Today we accept the basic principle that government is obligated to give a minimum amount of protection to those who are unable to meet their own needs. But regardless of governmental economic assistance to this segment of the population, there will always be a need for the voluntary agency, which can give best to the unfortunates the human love and warmth of spirit so vital to the individual.

In this regard, I am pleased to note that one of the purposes of the various diocesan organizations of Catholic Charities is not only to deal directly with individuals and families, but also to stimulate volunteer effort in connection with parish churches. This, I realize, is the fundamental purpose of the Society of St. Vincent De Paul, which is an important part of the National Conference of Catholic Charities. More and more, we must put Christianity into practice by recognizing the basic responsibility of every church member to be a "good Samaritan" and to give gladly personal services to others. I appreciate the fact that this organization is working along such lines in meeting welfare problems in the nation.

I am deeply concerned, as I know you are, over the breakdown of the home and family in American life. History shows that a nation decays when the home is neglected—such will be our tragic fate unless we take immediate steps to protect the home and family as the basic institutions of society.

A close study of the problem shows that the home and family are breaking down for several important reasons. One of them is the lack of spiritual life and training in the family. Millions of children are growing up in our country deprived of the benefits of religious teaching and example by their parents. The very survival of this nation depends upon our ability to gain the spiritual resources upon which we can draw in these perilous times. To help our children grow spiritually is the greatest task before us and one which we have miserably failed to cope with in this modern day.

Another blow to the home and family has been dealt by the growing apathy and absence of discipline on the part of the parents. The unity of the family is too often destroyed by the fact that its members have diverse interests that keep them away from the home. The home, in many cases, is nothing more than a dormitory. Too many parents are content to leave the inculcation of moral teaching, discipline and respect for law and order to the schools or the police or other agencies of government. Too many treat lightly their duty to their children to set good examples of respect for law and moral teachings. Too many parents are just too busy with outside interests of business or recreation to even get acquainted with their children. Because they have lost sight of the need for God, they fail to realize that there is no more important mission in life than that of rearing their children.

As a result of this failure to appreciate spiritual values and the importance of parental responsibility, we find an increasing number of divorces and separations. It is estimated that there are more than a million and a half children

with divorced parents in America today. Consider the trend
—in 1890 there was one divorce to every sixteen marriages
in the nation; in 1910, one divorce to every eleven marriages;
by 1940, it had increased to one divorce to six marriages;
today, it is said to be one divorce to every three marriages.
Some authorities believe that there will soon be one divorce
for every two marriages.

To study this growing problem, I recommended to the
Minnesota Legislature that a special commission be set up.
The Legislature accepted this suggestion and passed a law
which established this commission "to study the laws and
court organizations of Minnesota relating to juvenile courts,
and to domestic relations including divorce, separate maintenance, annulment of marriage, adoption, desertion, and non-
support." This commission is made up of a representative
group of well-qualified persons of all religious faiths. From
its studies, I am confident will come recommendations that
will help check this alarming tide of broken homes. But, most
important force of all in this effort, a resurgence of religious
faith in the home offers the greatest hope.

Catholic leaders and Catholic organizations were an essential part of our Youth Conservation program in Minnesota. The Bureau of Catholic Charities of St. Paul and the
Catholic Welfare Association of Minneapolis, as well as
state-wide participation of Catholic churches, contributed to
the success of our Youth Conference and are working hard
and ably in our coordinated effort to guide and assist the
youth of Minnesota.

Catholic groups are also performing outstanding service through wholehearted cooperation in our Minnesota Child
Placement Plan. In 1947 our child-caring agencies, both
public and private, reached this agreement: "Adoption is to

be considered for every child permanently severed from his natural family, for whom a suitable home can be found." This statement is now the heart of Minnesota placement policy. It means simply that adoption should be considered for all children in need of it—the older child, the physically-handicapped child, as well as the "normal" or "superior" infant.

Catholic agencies in Minnesota have accepted this premise that every child has the right to look forward to permanent placement in an adoptive home. In line with this thinking they have over the past years reduced the institutional population and helped make possible the outstanding success which our child placement program has achieved in the state.

Catholic agencies have also made a magnificent contribution to the progress of a relatively new type of service in Minnesota. I refer to the work of our Minnesota Commission on the Resettlement of Displaced Persons. Minnesota, I am told, was the first state to organize such a commission. We took this step months in advance of the passage of the National Displaced Persons Bill by Congress. We were determined to be ready to do our full share.

In choosing leaders to serve on the Commission, it was natural that we should look first to the churches. Here, above all else, was a program which was based upon our fundamental religious beliefs. It was an opportunity to show that we really practiced our religious philosophy and were willing to serve as the "good Samaritan" to our brothers in distress. The Fatherhood of God and the Brotherhood of Man were the logical cornerstones of a program aimed at the alleviation of human suffering. It was a glorious cause in which the Catholic, Jewish and Protestant churches were united in common interest. Representatives of all three faiths serve on the Commission and are contributing to its success.

Then, since our new residents and potential citizens must earn a living in our society, we asked leaders of organized labor to give counsel and assistance through service on the Commission. And to draw upon the experience and resources of the various state agencies, we added the State Director of Employment and Security, the State Director of Social Welfare, and the State Commissioner of Agriculture.

We take great pride in the accomplishments of our Commission. Since its inception, the Catholic Church has been ably represented on it by two of our outstanding churchmen and distinguished citizens—The Reverend Francis Curtin, Director of the St. Paul Bureau of Catholic Charities and Secretary of the Commission, and The Reverend James A. Byrnes, Pastor of The Annunciation Church in Minneapolis.

The Catholic Welfare Agency's enthusiastic response to and active support of the program is attested to by the fact that as of October 18, 1949, almost half—1236—of the 2528 displaced persons brought to Minnesota came under the auspices of the National Catholic Welfare Conference.

Our experience in the program to date is proof that the Catholic agency is sponsoring the type of people who will make fine American citizens. In our State Commission's role as coordinating and referral center for the several voluntary agencies in the resettlement program, we are able to receive information on most of the complaints arising from individual resettlement problems.

Of the more than 1200 Catholic persons brought to Minnesota, our Commission has received complaints or requests for assistance relating to only five of these placements—

less than one-half of one per cent. That is certainly an outstanding record when one considers the difficulties inherent in the nature of assurance requirements, the necessary delay, and the "sight-unseen" promises required of sponsors.

The small number of requests have been from displaced persons or interested citizens concerning problems of housing or employment. We have immediately referred these requests to the appropriate Catholic diocesan resettlement directors and in each case have received a prompt response and a report indicating that a satisfactory settlement has been, or is in the process of being worked out.

With this kind of cooperation, we feel assured of success in our ultimate objective for the program—which is the adjustment of the immigrant in the social and economic life of the communities of our state.

The displaced persons program has given us many benefits. Among them has been a splendid opportunity to show how well the voluntary agencies, with church affiliations, can meet a humanitarian problem such as that presented by these unfortunate people. Then, another important value has been the opportunity to have Catholic, Protestant and Jewish people working together for a common cause, and thus learning to know and respect one another more. These are precious gains for our state in the building of spiritual resources for the future.

It has been my policy to send a short letter of greeting and welcome to the displaced individuals shortly after their arrival in Minnesota. I want to tell you that those letters have brought responses which touch your heart. Never have I seen letters more filled with deep gratitude. They earnestly and fervently promise to become good citizens. I believe they will, and that they will contribute much to our state. I am most appreciative of the important role the Catholic Church has played in making this possible.

Some years ago it was my privilege to welcome the Midwest Conference on Displaced Persons as it began its sessions at our State Capitol in St. Paul. Out of that meeting developed, I feel, a new spirit of cooperation and coordination that will enable the Midwest group of states to do an even better job in the future in taking in displaced persons. We hope that Congress will take steps to liberalize the program so that we may early fulfill the responsibility that is ours to share our land and opportunities with these unfortunates.

In surveying the role of Catholic welfare work in Minnesota, I must touch upon another vital subject—that of breaking down the prejudice and bigotry which threatens our nation from within. In our state, we have a Governor's Interracial Commission which is designated as the agency to coordinate our activity in removing these blights from our democratic society through education and accurate information. The Commission is under the able chairmanship of The Reverend Francis J. Gilligan, a distinguished and brilliant Catholic leader, and his ability and enthusiasm have been a tremendous force in this important work.

This fight against prejudice is, I believe, one of the most effective means by which we can oppose atheistic communism and its evil program to stifle human liberty. For by wiping out religious and racial prejudice, we can build the kind of American unity and spirit which will be our strongest defense and give new heart to all who cherish freedom in this war-weary world.

CHAPTER XI

Chosen People of God

The Christian Church faces the most dangerous yet challenging mission in its entire history. In meeting this challenge, laymen must play a vital part.

We need to be constantly reminded of the role the laity has played in the Church since Jesus first chose the motley band of twelve from fishermen, tax collectors and ordinary folk. The very word "layman" springs from the Greek word "Laikos," meaning belonging to the people—that is the chosen people of God. In this framework of reference, all members of the Church are "laikoi."

The New Testament has a word for disciple—"Diakonia." In its original sense, this Greek word, Diakonia, means waiter on table. Jesus made this simple word with its humble origin the typical expression for the relation of his disciples with the world. It should be our cue for what we conceive to be the role of the layman in the mission of the Church. In this conviction we are fortified by Ephesians 4:11, which characterizes all Christians as being enlisted "for the upbuilding of the body of Christ."

St. John points up the role of the layman in the mission of the Church as he describes the scene in the upper room with Christ washing the disciples' feet. It is symbolic of what Christ expects of the laymen of the Church.

Laymen today are surrounded by a great host of witnesses as to their important mission in the work of the Church. St. Luke, the physician; St. Paul, the tent maker; Tertullian and St. Augustine—now listed among the great Church fathers, were all laymen. In the revolutionary movement in the middle ages, protesting against a too worldly church, recalling it to its true mission, we recall the lay movement of the Waldensians and the Lollards.

Martin Luther's reformation was mainly a lay movement with princes and peasants catching a new look at the role Christ intended the Church to play.

John Calvin, who fathered the Presbyterian Church, an extraordinarily gifted layman, stepped from a specialized study of jurisprudence into the movement recalling the Church to renewal.

America was cradled in a lay movement—recalling the Church to freedom of conscience and dignity of the common man. The Christian faith of the laymen who spearheaded this movement is attested by their complete reliance upon God to aid them in resolving their difficulties.

In our day, we need but mention such a name as Albert Schweitzer to be reminded of the role a layman can play in making the Christian faith relevant in the lives of men.

Moreover, we could call the roll of countless ordinary folk who are dedicating their lives in the witness and ministry of the Church. My church recently called a production foreman from a lucrative position in a Caterpillar plant and sent him to the untouchables of India. He will teach the use of tools and open employment for a people to whom, heretofore, were open only menial jobs. This is a ministry of sharing under the leadership of a layman. This, too, dramatizes the relevancy of the mission of the Church in world affairs.

This age of space in which we live demands an articulate, aggressive and dedicated laymanship. Doubt, despair and deterioration of our personal and public life appear beneath the thin veneer of our society—and this despite the unprecedented Church and Sunday School attendance and accelerated building of church plants.

The real difference between the Soviet system and our system is that we profess that we are, and strive to live as a nation under God, and yet there are ominous signs we are straying from the path.

What's wrong? The torch of religion may be lit in the Church, but it is not burning as it should in the family, in the shop, or on the street. Democracy is in trouble today and only the Christian heritage can revitalize it.

We have been too smug and complacent about the freedom we have enjoyed. Because we had it yesterday, and have it today, many have assumed we will have it tomorrow. But the events of the last few years ought to awaken us from our lethargy.

Eleven years ago I was privileged, while Governor of Minnesota, to accompany General Clay and others in the historic mission to Berlin for the ringing of the world's Freedom Bell. On United Nation's Day, October 25, 1950, the peal of that great bell was sent behind the iron curtain to signify that the forces of democracy were dedicated to the idea that this world, under God, should have a new birth of freedom.

In October, 1960, I stood on the border between Czechoslovakia and the Western Zone of Germany—the border between slavery and freedom.

Once again I was privileged to accompany the Crusade for Freedom group which went to Lisbon, Munich and Berlin to inspect Radio Free Europe facilities and to commemorate the tenth anniversary of the ringing of the world's Freedom Bell.

Army helicopters took us to the Czechoslovakian border where we saw the Soviet guards in a tower behind the electrically charged barbed wire fences peering at us through field glasses. We were American spies, according to Tass News Agency.

Even the grass dramatically emphasized the dividing line. Grass was green on freedom's side and bleak and dead on slavery's side!

Every member of the Crusade for Freedom group came away with the deep conviction that we have to be willing to sacrifice more and pay a greater price than we have been paying to insure that we shall continue to be free.

We cannot afford to take a chance to win the struggle with the Soviets only in the economic, political or military fields. We still must press forward, of course, in these fields and we have faith that the Soviets will not be able to excel us economically, politically or militarily; but it is in the moral and spiritual realm that we have a real chance for victory, and only as we continue to live under God will we have a chance to remain free. A revival of the dynamic faith that sparked the revolution is imperative.

Christianity has not failed so far. We laymen have failed to understand the true significance of the role of the layman in the mission of the Church.

We have failed to put Christianity into practice in our daily experiences. Too many of us have been unwilling to pay the price for it.

We have failed to put it into practice in our homes. That is why one of every three marriages terminates in divorce and juvenile delinquency is an acute problem.

We have failed to put it into practice in our very churches in many instances. That is why we have disunity and ineffectiveness in much of our work.

We have failed to put it into practice in management-labor relations. That is why we have collusive arrangements between management and labor and abuses on both sides to the detriment of the public.

We have failed to put it into practice in politics and government. That is why we have influence peddling, corruption of public officials, disregard and disrespect for law.

We have failed to put it into practice in our treatment of minority groups—that is why we have race riots, intolerance and bigotry.

We have failed to put it into practice in our international relations—that is why we have war.

In all these great areas of human relations we, as Christian laymen, have the opportunity to effect a miraculous change in affairs by practicing Christianity in setting an example for the rest of the people who do not believe, or who pay only lip service to the teachings of Jesus.

But there are those within our Churches, and they are sincere and well-meaning, who proclaim that religion and politics do not mix; that the purpose of the Church is to preach the Gospel and its business is not to be concerned with the social issues of the day.

Mr. Dahlberg, the former dynamic President of the National Council of Churches of Christ, has effectively answered this contention. Courageously he has stated that the prophetic voice of the Church will not be silenced; that pastors and laymen, alike, are compelled to interpret the Gospel in terms of the moral and spiritual issues of our time; and that it is the responsibility of the Church to speak out on these issues even before they become political issues.

On many occasions during my administration as Governor of Minnesota, when I was fighting for honesty and humanity in government; in eliminating the slot machine racket; in providing for humane care for mentally ill, and other programs, I told our Church people, "We get just as bad government as we are willing to stand for and just as good government as we are willing to fight for." And I will say to the credit of the Church people of Minnesota, when they were finally aroused out of their apathy and indifference, **they became militant crusaders** in helping us achieve these programs for better government.

If government is corrupt, inefficient and unprogressive, it is because Christian people have not sufficiently cared. On the other hand, if government is honest, humane, and progressive, it is because Christian people are alert to their citizenship responsibilities.

The Christian citizen must dedicate himself to a program that places human values first. He must fight for honesty and humanity in government. As Christ was most concerned with children and unfortunates, so must the Christian citizen see that government invests generously in education, health, and general welfare of youth. He must fight for humane care of the mentally ill and other fellow human beings in need of a helping hand. He must set an example of self-discipline and wholesome respect for law and order and fight vigorously for honesty and integrity in public life. He must work to put Christianity into practice by striving to foster and protect the heritage of citizenship for all of every creed, race and national origin. We laymen need the urgency of mission that was the mark of the Master.

Channing Pollock, in speaking of the world's slow stain, states,

"America, above all other nations, needs a better understanding of what failure really is. Most of us know pretty well by instinct what is best in ourselves. Insofar as we turn away from that through hope of reward or dread of penalty, we are smeared with the world's stain. Judas with his thirty pieces of silver was a failure. Christ on the cross was the greatest figure of time and eternity."

We must rediscover the role of the laity in the mission of the Church. Part of the laity's responsibility, of course, is to operate the institutional machinery of the Church.

But in the dynamic Biblical sense, laity are the people of God abroad in the world. Laypeople in various segments of society are God's messengers for the releasing of grace and power for the healing of human life. As Luther put it, they are called upon to be little Christs.

Real Christians are the ones who are doing things, not just talking about doing things. Jesus was an activist in the

best and well-balanced sense of that word. Thirty-three short
years, but what years!

Henry Ward Beecher once spoke of men who thought
that the object of conversion was to clean them as a gar-
ment is cleaned and that when they were converted they were
to be hung up in the Lord's wardrobe, the door of which was
to be shut so that no dust could get at them. A coat that is not
used, contended Beecher, the moths eat, and a Christian who
is hung up so that he shall not be tempted—the moths eat
him, and they have poor food at that.

When one has been touched by Jesus, the place for him
is out among others, amid the turmoil of life, expressing by
his words and deeds what his faith has meant to him. He is
to be a commissioned ambassador—a living example all the
time.

We pay tribute to God's ministers who have answered
the call to service in His kingdom. But I am sure they will
be the first to admit that witness and ministry are not restricted to men specially ordained or to places particularly consecrated.

The politician, the worker, the professional man, and the
merchant are also God's ministers, and their places of witness and ministry are in the market place, the shops and in
public affairs. Laymen and ministers, alike, are called by
God to the service of Jesus Christ.

It is related that shortly after the last war, an American
army outfit was given the task of reconstructing a small German village which had been practically demolished by bombs.
With customary American efficiency, they rebuilt the village.
As they were reconstructing a small church, they had completed their task, except for a statue of Christ. Search as they

would, they could not find the hands of the statue and they seemed to be in a dilemma. Finally the captain of the contingent, who had been an active layman in the church, said, "I know what we will do; we will inscribe these words on the base of the statue: 'I have no other hands than yours.' " This illustrates, of course, that the Gospel of Christ can be disseminated only through His followers—the lay people of our Churches.

Laymen must answer the question, "What does it mean to be a Christian physician, professional man, business man, farmer, worker, or executive?"

The answer must be that the Christian Gospel is relevant to every concrete issue of life. Too often has the Church been insensitive to the world in which it lives.

What a different Church it would be if it would frankly and aggressively challenge the modern paganism of our times. Yet that is the genus of our Christian heritage.

The missionary apostles in the early years of the Church, as they preached in the market places of Corinth, the forum in Rome, or the wilderness of medieval Europe, did not hesitate to hurl that type of challenge to their listeners.

America was founded by men who were bold. It cannot be maintained by men who are timid. The Church must have leadership and programs in rethinking our ministry to the world.

Christianity is desperately in need of lay members who will give more than half-loyalty, secret discipleship and lukewarm fealty or lip service. Clearly the lines are being drawn for a struggle between the Church of Jesus Christ and the Godless materialism that would destroy men's souls. Leadership in this great moral struggle must come only from a revitalized Church.

The spiritual victories will be won where laymen live and work. In the family, in politics, in finance, racial relationship, in community service, and in the Church itself.

The world and its thought has not been sufficiently influenced by Christian testimony. The demand of the hour is that the voice of the Church will penetrate far more into the current scene. Laymen must be courageous in speaking out, no matter what the cost or risk, on issues and problems which intimately concern the men of our time.

Through the teaching of Christianity we can build a world of humanity and justice and banish the evil forces of greed that foment war.

This is the road we must follow. Protestant Churches have a major contribution to make in the spiritual revival of our time which must come quickly if civilization is to be saved from impending doom. This space age demands a new reformation—a spiritual renaissance.

True, it is a day of crises. But "crisis"—compounded out of two Chinese characters—means first, danger; second, opportunity. There is danger and there are many perplexing problems, but what an opportunity! The intriguing frontier of human values and human relations is yet to be explored.

Communism and every anti-Christian movement is demanding a wholehearted devotion and a loyalty bravely proclaimed. Nothing less will suffice for this generation of Christians.

Sincere, fiery and zealous devotion must displace the half-loyalty and lukewarm fealty so characteristic of many Christians of this day.

Never has there been a greater need for Christians in all areas of life to come out boldly and without reservation in a united consecration for the common good of all.

Today the man who does not declare his loyalty to Christ is no more than an onlooker—a neutral in the face of Christianity's greatest test in all history.

The faith of the early Christians was so daring that the threat of death could not stop them. Faith today has lost much of this daring. This space age demands that laymen of the Church get off the launching pad of apathy, indifference and half-loyalty, into the area of a vigorous, dynamic and daring Christian faith that will send them into the market places of life as disciplined and courageous Christians ready to face the issues of the day.

Too many people are drifting through life insecure, filled with worries and tensions. Getting back to God and finding a philosophy of life that places selfish desires secondary to Christian service is the task meriting top priority in America today.

Great, proud America, with seemingly limitless natural resources, mighty in war and in peace, has, it so often seems, lost sight of God. We have deluded ourselves into believing that we are self-sufficient and require no aid from a power above ourselves.

Religious faith has guided our nation through many stormy days. We must rely upon Christianity to sustain us now in the most crucial test of all, for no scientific discovery or increased material resources can make good the spiritual deficit which endangers man in this age.

God waits silently and patiently for us to accept the salvation He holds out to us. O blind and insecure America, awake, look up. These are days which require a purpose and mission and an abiding faith to carry us over the rocky, treacherous road ahead. Christ alone stands ready to give us this help and to guide us safely through the hazardous stretches of time.

> *"He has sounded forth the trumpet that has*
> *never called retreat.*
> *He is sifting out the hearts of men before*
> *His judgment seat.*
> *O be swift my soul to answer Him,*
> *Be jubilant, my feet,*
> *Our God is marching on!"*

CHAPTER XII

The Rule of Law

We live under the rule of law. We choose to do so because man has learned through experience that argument before an unbiased tribunal is far the better way to settle disputes than a system where arguments are settled by individual assertions of power with the decision to the strongest.

The supreme law of our land is the Constitution. This is so because our Nation began with the ratification of this document by nine states, by the acceptance of the Constitution by each and every state that entered the Union thereafter, and by reason of the second sentence of Article VI of the Constitution which states that the Constitution shall be the "supreme law of the Land."

There has been much discussion in recent years about the Constitution; much argument about the powers it bestows and those it withholds.

Basically, the system of government established by it is one of federalism. By this is meant a dual form of government—one by each of the states and one by the federal government in Washington. In establishing the central government, the designers of the Constitution delegated to it only those powers on which national uniformity was or might be necessary. Matters of local concern were left to the state. However, both in the Constitution as originally drafted, and in subsequent amendments, there are provisions limiting the discretion of the states in connection with matters which were not otherwise put within the purview of the national government. One of these restrictions is at the basis of the controversy raging today over segregation in the public schools. It is the 14th Amendment and it is the severest restraint on the states. This amendment reads in part:

"No State shall . . . deny to any person within its jurisdiction the equal protection of the laws."

What this phrase means and the function of the Supreme Court in ascertaining such meaning is a pressing problem we are faced with today.

In its simplest terms, the amendment abolishes class legislation. That is, no state may unjustly discriminate against any person or group of persons. The problem arises when an attempt is made to apply this formula to a concrete fact situation. In 1954, the Supreme Court had before it the question of whether segregation of the races in the public schools of four states violated the 14th Amendment; the Court decided that it did, and the repercussions of that decision are still being felt.

The Fourteenth Amendment became a part of our Constitution in 1868. The history of segregation in the public schools since that date has had three phases.

The first stage lasted from 1868 to 1896. During that time there was little litigation on the question. In those states that practiced segregation the controlling rule was that so long as the facilities afforded Negroes were equal to those afforded whites, there was no denial of "equal protection of the laws."

The constitutionality of this "separate but equal" doctrine first came before the Supreme Court in 1896 in the now famous case of *Plessy v. Ferguson*. Plessy, a one-eighth Negro, entered a railroad car reserved for whites. He refused to go to the coach reserved for Negroes and so was arrested and convicted under a Louisiana statute making such action criminal. When he brought his case to the Supreme Court of the United States, that Court upheld his conviction on the ground that this segregation law did not violate the Fourteenth Amendment since the "separate" facilities were "equal."

One Justice dissented. For him, the Constitution was "color-blind." Justice Harlan wrote:

> "(I)n view of the Constitution, in the eye of the law, there is in this country no superior, dominant, ruling class of citizens. There is no caste here. Our Constitution is color-blind, and neither knows nor tolerates classes among citizens. In respect of civil rights, all citizens are equal before the law."

But this opinion was in dissent. The seven other Justices on the Court who heard the case held the "separate but equal" doctrine constitutional. Thus began the second phase.

In 1927, the Supreme Court, in a unanimous decision, applied the principle of "separate but equal" to public schools. A nine-year-old girl of Chinese descent was refused admission to a Mississippi school for white children. Her father brought suit to compel the school authorities to admit the child; they refused and the Court upheld their refusal. Again it was said that "separate but equal" facilities did not violate the Fourteenth Amendment's guarantee to all persons of "equal protection of the laws."

Beginning in December, 1938, the Court began to re-
examine the doctrine. In cases dealing with education in professional schools, an inquiry was made to determine whether
equality in the separate facilities actually existed. Thus, in
Missouri ex rel. Gaines v. Canada, the Court held that Lloyd
Gaines, a Negro, was entitled to admission into Missouri's
law school. Missouri's practice had been to pay the tuition
fees for Missouri Negroes in law schools of nearby states,
rather than provide for a separate law school for Negroes
in Missouri. This system, said the Supreme Court in 1938,
violated the Fourteenth Amendment. Later cases applied this
to Oklahoma, which had no separate law school, and Texas
and Louisiana, which had separate schools but not substantially equal ones.

In 1950, the Court seriously narrowed the "separate but
equal" doctrine when it held that a Negro graduate student,
in the University of Oklahoma, named McLaurin, had been
denied equality of treatment with whites. McLaurin had been
admitted to the same classroom, the same library and the
same cafeteria that the white students used. But in each of
these parts of the school, he had been required to sit at a
designated place and this, said the Court, was unjust discrimination. Thus, even though he heard the same lectures,
could use the same books and could eat the same food as
the whites, the Court held that he had been denied the equal
protection of the laws. Mr. Chief Justice Vinson said of this
type of Southern "equality":

> ". . . they signify that the State, in administering the
> facilities it affords for professional and graduate
> study, sets McLaurin apart from the other students.
> The result is that appellant is handicapped in his pur-
> suit of effective graduate instruction. Such restric-

tions impair and inhibit his ability to study, to engage in discussions and exchange views with other students, and, in general, to learn his profession."

It should be pointed out here that during these years a powerful ally of the "equal protection of the laws" guarantee was also at work. This is the clause in the eighth section of Article I of the Constitution that gives to Congress the sole power to regulate interstate commerce. By resort to this, the Court held, in 1946, that a Virginia statute which required the separation of white and colored passengers on commercial vehicles was invalid as applied to a passenger in interstate travel. *Plessy v. Ferguson* was not mentioned.

Once again, cases dealing with segregation in the public schools began to form. Eventually, cases from Kansas, South Carolina, Virginia and Delaware were consolidated for argument before the Supreme Court. And this is a notable feature of the Segregation Cases. The Court was careful to delay the hearing of this important question until it would be presented with records and arguments of a fair cross-section of the country, not just of one state.

The South Carolina case was first docketed in the 1951 October Term; it was sent back in January, 1952, for reconsideration by the District Court. The effect was to delay Supreme Court consideration until the 1952 Term, by which time appeals had been filed in the Kansas and Virginia cases. The Court then officially recognized a segregation case pending in the Court of Appeals for the District of Columbia and informed the parties that the Court would be willing to hear the case—an unusual step, but in line with the Court's desire to hear all the cases simultaneously. The Delaware case was added a month later.

Finally, in the October Term of 1952, the Court heard arguments on the five cases, but no decision was given. Instead, re-argument was ordered for the October Term, 1953. When the Court finally ruled on the cases, it gave further evidence of its desire for careful consideration of all the factors involved. It decided initially only the substantive issue presented, and directed all interested parties to prepare for future argument on the decree to be formulated to guide resolution of the problems of each segregated school district.

The decision on the constitutional issue was handed down on May 17, 1954. The "separate but equal" doctrine was abolished. Chief Justice Warren, speaking for a unanimous Court, said:

"To separate them from others of similar age and qualifications solely because of their race generates a feeling of inferiority as to their status in the community that may affect their hearts and minds in a way unlikely ever to be undone. The effect of this separation on their educational opportunities was well stated by a finding in the Kansas case by a court which nevertheless felt compelled to rule against the Negro plaintiffs: 'Segregation of white and colored children in public schools has a detrimental effect upon the colored children. The impact is greater when it has the sanction of the law; for the policy of separating the races is usually interpreted as denoting the inferiority of the Negro group. A sense of inferiority affects the motivation of a child to learn. Segregation with the sanction of law, therefore, has a tendency to retard the educational and mental development of Negro children and to deprive them of some of the benefits they would receive in a racially integrated school system.' "

The Chief Justice then went on to say:

"Whatever may have been the extent of psychological knowledge at the time of Plessy v. Ferguson, this finding is amply supported by modern authority. Any language in Plessy v. Ferguson contrary to this finding is rejected. We conclude that in the field of public education the doctrine of 'separate but equal' has no place. Separate education facilities are inherently unequal."

Having traced the history of this decision, it can be seen how gradual the transformation was. Indeed, it might almost be said that it followed along as our knowledge of the effects of segregation grew, and consequently as our knowledge of the meaning of the word "equal" in the Fourteenth Amendment grew. And the gradual adjustment that the Court called for is evident from the decree rendered one year later, May 31, 1955.

Chief Justice Warren, again for a unanimous court, ordered that the district courts would grant the relief "because of their proximity to local conditions and the possible need for further hearings." He then went on to say:

"In fashioning and effectuating the decrees, the courts will be guided by equitable principles . . . While giving weight to these public and private considerations, the courts will require that the defendants make a prompt and reasonable start toward full compliance with our May 17, 1954, ruling. Once such a start has been made, the courts may find that additional time is necessary to carry out the ruling in an effective manner. The burden rests upon the defendants to establish that such time is necessary in the public interest and is consistent with good faith compliance at the earliest practicable date."

Thus began the third phase in the history of segregation in public schools—a phase that the Supreme Court ushered in with restrained language and a plea to reason for good faith compliance.

In the years since then, many cases have been decided. There is no necessity to discuss each of them; suffice it to say that in some the School Boards were found to have failed to comply with the Supreme Court's decree of 1955, and in some—and this is significant—it was found that the School Boards were making a good faith compliance with the decree, so that pleas for speedier desegregation were denied.

The most important decision on how much time School Boards were to be allowed and what reasons constituted justification for delay came in the Little Rock case. The question presented was whether delay could be had in order to avoid conflict and unrest and to attempt to gain public acceptance of desegregation. The answer by the unanimous Court—and really the only answer—can be found in the opinion of the Court in 1955 in which the original decrees were formulated:

> "(I)t should go without saying that the vitality of these constitutional principles cannot be allowed to yield simply because of disagreement with them."

Has the Supreme Court been wrong in rendering these decisions? Have the Justices ignored the fundamental maxim of our system of government, that it is "a government of laws, not men"? Have they acted as a "third legislative chamber"? Have they amended our Constitution on their own?

To answer these questions, to determine just what the function of the Supreme Court is, we must turn to the Constitution.

The Constitution says simply that "the Judicial Power of the United States shall be vested in one Supreme Court, and in such inferior Courts as the Congress may from time to time ordain and establish." The Constitution itself gives the Supreme Court authority to hear cases at their inception only where the case involves a foreign diplomat or is one to which a state is a party. In all other cases encompassed by the term "judicial power" the Supreme Court has authority only to review decisions of the state and lower federal courts —and this latter authority is subject to "such Exceptions, and under such Regulations as the Congress shall make." As for the "inferior Federal courts" they are creatures of Congress, and exist only at the will of Congress.

Thus there is no provision in the Constitution explicitly authorizing the Supreme Court to review the decisions of lower courts to determine whether they comport with the Constitution. However, as Chief Justice Marshall recognized in 1803 in the celebrated case of *Marbury v. Madison,* such review is required if the place of the Constitution as the supreme law of the land is to be maintained. As Marshall indicated, to provide that the Constitution is to be supreme law and that the courts are to review "all cases arising under the Constitution," and yet say at the same time that laws conflicting with the Constitution shall be enforced by the courts, is not only inconsistent but would "subvert the very foundation of all written constitutions." To fulfill their duty of upholding the Constitution, judges must strike down all laws inconsistent with it.

Therefore, the Supreme Court has the power to interpret the Constitution—no one denies this. But the authority is just this—to interpret. The Court is not to graft new law onto the provisions of the Constitution—either by altering or ignoring the language of these provisions.

When we read the Constitution we see that there are many terms in it that are very general and unspecific. These must, of necessity, "gather meaning from experience," as Justice Frankfurter has written. The few provisions that are explicit are, for the most part, uncontroversial, with their meaning apparent on their face. Thus, there is no room for interpretation of the provision in Section 1 of Article II that the President "shall hold his Office during the Term of four Years." Nor need we speculate on what is meant by the language in Section 2 of Article I that "No Person shall be a Representative who shall not have attained to the Age of twenty-five Years." But what of the great concepts in the Constitution? What of such terms as "due process of law," "liberty," "property" and "equal protection of the laws"? It is here that the Supreme Court serves its function. Whether you think it serves it properly depends on which of two philosophies you accept. The first was well stated by Mr. Justice Sutherland in a dissent in the case of *Home Building & Loan Association v. Blaisdell.*

"The whole aim of construction, as applied to a provision of the Constitution, is to discover the meaning, to ascertain and give effect to the intent, of its framers and the people who adopted it . . . As nearly as possible we should place ourselves in the condition of those who framed and adopted it."

Chief Justice Hughes in the same case, for the majority, explicitly rejected that philosophy and presented the alternative:

"If by the statement that what the Constitution meant at the time of its adoption it means today, it is intended to say that the great clauses of the Constitution must be confined to the interpretation which the framers, with the conditions and outlook of their time, would have placed upon them, the statement carries its own refutation. It was to guard against such a narrow conception that Chief Justice Marshall uttered the memorable warning—'we must never forget that it is *a constitution* we are expounding' . . ."

Justice McKenna had this attitude in mind in *Weems v. United States*. In that case, the Court held that a fine plus imprisonment for fifteen years for violating a Philippine statute by corruptly making false entries in public records constituted cruel and unusual punishment within the meaning of the Eighth Amendment and hence also within the meaning of the Philippine Bill of Rights. Speaking to the argument that the Court was applying the Eighth Amendment in circumstances in which its framers might not have thought it applicable, Justice McKenna said, in a frequently quoted passage:

"Time works changes, brings into existence new conditions and purposes. Therefore a principle to be vital must be capable of wider application than the mischief which gave it birth. This is peculiarly true of constitutions. They are not ephemeral enactments, designed to meet passing occasions . . . The future is their care and provision for events of good and bad tendencies of which no prophecy can be made. In the application of a constitution, therefore, our contemplation cannot be only of what has been but of what may be. Under any other rule a constitution would indeed be as easy of application as it would be deficient in efficacy and power. Its general principles would have little value and be converted by precedent into impotent and lifeless formulas."

Here, then, we have pinpointed the conflict. Sixty-two years ago, the Supreme Court said that government facilities that are separate for the races can still be "equal" within the meaning of the Fourteenth Amendment. Yet the Supreme Court of 1954 decided that if government facilities are separate they are inherently unequal.

Segregationists feel this change in the interpretation of the Fourteenth Amendment constitutes an unwarranted intervention of the Supreme Court into the field of legislation; that in breaking from precedent, the Supreme Court broke immutable law.

But ever since our nation was organized, the Supreme Court has broken from precedent when the times demanded. The very same Justices who decided the Plessy case recognized this. In a case decided one year earlier, in 1895, they said:

> "We are sensible of the great weight to which (a previous decision) is entitled. But at the same time we are convinced that, if we follow it, we follow an erroneous decision into which the court fell, when the great importance of the question as it now presents itself could not be foreseen. . . .

> "Manifestly, as this court is clothed with the power, and entrusted with the duty, to maintain the fundamental law of the Constitution, the discharge of that duty requires it not to extend any decision upon a constitutional question if it is convinced that error in principle might supervene."

And how realistic this attitude is. There must never be a rigid adherence to precedent. If change could not be made, child labor would still be with us; we would have no laws setting forth minimum wages and maximum hours; mentally ill persons would be treated no differently than anyone else in a criminal trial.

Can we say that "liberty" means the same thing now that it meant in 1787 when today an Internal Revenue agent, upon showing his credentials, can lawfully demand to inspect a person's business books and records? Can we say that "freedom of contract" means the same thing now that it meant in 1787 when we apply it to the hiring of children? Does "interstate commerce" today mean what it meant in 1787— when it took as long to travel from Washington to Baltimore as it now does to cross the country?

If these terms have altered in meaning, they have done so because of the fantastic change in our society. Our judges must be aware of the change and apply the new understanding.

It is specious to say that the change may be desirable but it must come from the legislature, and not the courts. It is specious because the job of making these kinds of changes in constitutional interpretation as conditions change is, as indicated previously, one which the Constitution has given the Courts. If it is desired that the task be taken from the courts, the remedy is constitutional amendment. I think, though, that on reflection the vast majority of our citizens will not desire such an amendment—that they will recognize that the task of interpreting the Constitution must be placed somewhere in our governmental structure, and that it is best placed in the hands of carefully trained and selected judges free from the swaying passions of political struggles.

Reflective citizens presented with the argument that change in a matter like segregation should be made by local

legislatures will also recognize that from a practical standpoint, such changes do not come forth from such quarters.

Now to say that the Court should not be bound by the
original understanding of the constitutional provision in
question is not to say that the original understanding is ir-
relevant.

The Court recognized this and in ordering a re-argument
in Brown in 1953, it asked the attorneys to discuss the understanding of the Fourteenth Amendment at the time of its enactment. The Court's conclusion, after hearing the arguments
and studying the briefs filed, was that the intention of the
framers was "inconclusive." Just as the Constitution itself
was the product of compromise, so, too, the Fourteenth
Amendment was the product of compromise. Language was
chosen that was general; that would be acceptable enough
to enable its passage; that would leave to the courts the appli-
cability of the amendment to the question of segregation in
the public schools.

In light of this, Chief Justice Warren wrote, in 1954:

> "In approaching this problem, we cannot turn the
> clock back to 1868 when the Amendment was adopt-
> ed, or even to 1896 when *Plessy v. Ferguson* was writ-
> ten. We must consider public education in the light
> of its full development and its present place in Amer-
> ican life throughout the Nation. Only in this way can
> it be determined if segregation in public schools de-
> prives these plaintiffs of the equal protection of the
> laws."

That is, the Court said that since the original understanding was that the courts should have the task of molding the
amendment to suit the times, that is just what the Court would
do—it would not abdicate its function.

In reaching its decision that segregation was unconstitutional, the Court resorted to sociological and psychological treatises. This has been severely condemned. But whenever the courts must make a decision in an area where the law governs social relationships the judges must, of necessity, consider the knowledge concerning those social relationships. And as our knowledge grows, so, too, must the law. This is not "judicial legislation." It is what the courts have always done. Is it not a little strange to suggest that judges should be forbidden to read books on sociology and psychology so that their minds will not receive knowledge outside the "judicial" sphere? What we need are judges who understand the new disciplines and who do *not* lose touch with the world around them.

All this is not to say that there are no limits as to how far the courts may go to reflect in their opinions the growth of our knowledge and the change in circumstances. The line is a wavering one but doctrine and principles have grown up to help define it.

If courts do happen to wander past this line—and it is not suggested that such was the case in the Segregation Cases —the solution is not to take away their jurisdiction. This form of "penalty," so vehemently proposed in the 85th Congress, is, in the last analysis, constitutional suicide. Moreover, it would probably be unsuccessful—just as past assaults on the Court have usually been unsuccessful. The late Justice Robert Jackson said:

"Public opinion . . . seems always to sustain the power of the Court, even against attack by popular executives and even though the public more than once has repudiated particular decisions. It is inescapable in our form of government that authority exists somewhere to interpret an instrument which sets up our whole structure and defines the powers of the Federal Government. . . . The people have seemed to feel that the Supreme Court, whatever its defects, is still the most detached, dispassionate, and trustworthy custodian that our system affords for the translation of abstract into concrete constitutional commands."

In this we find the solution. Only in continued constructive criticism of the Court's work and an insistence upon the appointment of men of ability will our country be aided. But it must be borne in mind that there is a great distinction between constructive criticism and disrespectful disobedience. There is no room for the latter.

A frequent charge by critics of the Supreme Court is that the Court has been power-hungry — deciding cases even though the traditional doctrines called for an exercise of judicial self-restraint. In isolated cases, there may be validity to this charge; with reference to the way the Supreme Court has conducted itself through the years, the charge would appear to be without merit.

For example, one of the first actions by the Supreme Court was its refusal to give President Washington advice regarding construction of treaties, laws of nations, and other laws of the land. Speaking for the Court, Chief Justice John Jay invoked the doctrine of separation of powers to restrict the Court's area of action to resolution of concrete cases. In thus refraining from issuance of "advisory opinions" on abstract questions—a practice still adhered to—the Court severely limited its ability to "grab power."

Another example of the Court's refusal to assume or retain power where not consistent with the Constitution was its decision, in 1938, to overturn a ninety-six-year-old precedent which held that federal district courts—and ultimately itself on review—possessed the power to declare a federal common law in suits between citizens of different states. Instead, said the Court, the Constitution, as properly interpreted, required that state law be applied in such cases.

The Court has also denied itself power by certain rules of construction which it utilizes in considering cases—chiefly those which attempt, if possible, to avoid deciding cases on a constitutional basis if statutory grounds for decision can be relied on. In this way the Court avoids placing the Constitution as a barrier to new legislative attempts to alter the statutes it interprets. Thus, of the recent cases causing the most controversy today, only the Segregation Cases were put on a constitutional basis.

The *Nelson* case, in which the Court invalidated a Pennsylvania anti-subversive statute, was based on the Court's conclusion that Congress, in passing the Federal Smith Act, had expressed the intention that the Federal Government have the exclusive job of prosecuting subversion of the Nation. The Supreme Court's ruling in that case, incidentally, affirmed the decision of the Pennsylvania Supreme Court.

Likewise, the *Mallory* ruling that confessions made by arrested individuals during periods of "unnecessary delay" between their arrest and their appearance before a magistrate to be advised of their rights was an interpretation of a Congressionally-approved rule of evidence.

Other cases could be cited beyond these to indicate that the Court's decisions, if read with an open mind, do not support its indictment as a "power-grabber."

Rather these cases and, in fact, the actions of the entire judiciary should reveal that the courts recognize their responsibility to play only the role which the Constitution assigns them; that they appreciate, as Alexander Hamilton indicated in the 78th number of the Federalist, that their lack of control of the "sword or purse" or of the "wealth of society generally . . . proves incontestably that the judiciary is beyond comparison the weakest of the three branches of power"; and that

> ". . . their power and influence rests solely upon the appeal for the assertion and protection of rights guaranteed by the Constitution and by the laws of the land and on the confidence reposed in the soundness of their decisions and the purity of their motives."

I am confident that the judiciary will continue to recognize these principles in the years to come.

Chapter XIII

Our Liberty and a Fearless Judiciary

As though safeguarding our very heritage, there stands before the Archives of the United States in Washington, D. C., overlooking Constitution Avenue, a statue of a classic warrior, sword in one hand, helmet in the other. At the base of this striking figure are inscribed the time-honored yet robust words,

ETERNAL VIGILANCE IS THE PRICE OF LIBERTY.

This statue symbolizes one of the reasons for the vast energies which are expended day after day by so many who labor in behalf of our nation.

To me the statue is a reminder of the continuing obligation imposed upon all of us as citizens to foster within our great democracy an active and working concern for individual liberty. It is a stern admonition that the preservation of freedom is a never-ending task.

The delicate balance between freedom and order is being upset continuously by the ceaseless conflict of political, economic, and social forces. The job of maintaining the proper democratic balance can never end. The condition we must strive to create is an atmosphere in which each of us feels so secure that our full potential is liberated and we are able to channel our resources in pursuit of the goals we covet, without undue external direction, compulsion, restriction or inhibition. In large measure this responsibility must be carried by men of the bar and the bench, equipped as we are, or ought to be, through our training and professional activity to weigh conflicting data with delicate precision and imagination. We must be alert to act as levellers when hostile ideology or nation, by threatening the mutual security of us all, throws society into such unreasoning turmoil that unnecessary and excessive repression of individual freedom is not only overlooked, is not only tolerated, but is even demanded as a social good.

My position has always been and remains quite simple. We are a democracy. The underlying principles of a democracy are not tumbleweeds which can be blown every which way by the climate of the times, or by the whim of any person or group of people. The freedom of American society is an ordered freedom, a freedom under God and under the law. We call the rights of our citizens *inalienable* precisely because men are not endowed with them by other men but, in the words of the Declaration of Independence, "by their Creator."

It cannot be repeated too often that the lifeblood of democracy is the belief that there is something of supreme worth in every human being. Every individual is the central point in the measure of value. Every individual has the right to be treated as unique and precious. No individual can be considered a generally expendable entity. No individual has the right to consider or conduct himself as though his life and liberty were more important than those of others, regardless of existing differences in the talents, capabilities, virtues or beliefs among men.

It must follow that liberty and freedom are desirable because the freedom to make choices and to act upon them is crucial to the development of those faculties that make one a human being. Take away his ability to select good from bad, circumscribe too tightly his talent for making rational choices, and man is no better than other animals. Only by making use of our freedom do we develop the human qualities of self-restraint and responsibility. Only where it exists can we exploit our full capacity for growth. In the free exercise of these faculties comes social progress and the greater the freedom the greater the probability that better ways of living will be discovered.

In the final analysis, the source of all government power in America is, and must remain, in the people. Ours is a limited government created by the people to promote the welfare of the people. In the words of Ralph Waldo Emerson: "The office of America is to liberate."

I think that most Americans recognize what I have said and believe all this. And yet we are constantly involved in quarrels over the nature of our liberties. This is inevitable. No liberty is limitless. Some liberties conflict with other liberties. Some liberties seem to threaten other values we hold equally dear, such as the safety of our nation. So veneration of liberties in the abstract is not enough. The real test is what we do about concrete cases. The strength of our democracy rests in large measure upon the conduct of the judiciary in handling these individual cases.

Currently there remain challenges to the judiciary which must be met if, as an institution, it is to be both independent and true to the promise of the Magna Charta:

"To no one will we sell, to no one will we refuse, or delay, right of justice . . . No . . . man shall be taken or imprisoned, or outlawed, or exiled, or anywise destroyed: nor shall we go upon him nor send upon him, but by the lawful judgment of his peers or by the law of the land."

In America, unlike totalitarian nations, the judiciary is not an organ of state power. Its position, as its responsibility, was stated well by Senator Alexander Wiley when he was Chairman of the Senate Judiciary Committee:

"An independent judiciary is a strong judiciary, a fearless judiciary, having respect for its co-equal branches of Government, but respecting even more its paramount obligation to the American people in interpreting the supreme law of the land."

Our commission is to see that it does not fall short of these standards.

Fast upon the heels of the Second World War a security psychosis gripped our land. With the constant and erratic shifts in policy by the communist nations, many of our people were seized with the panic of pregnability. Many capitulated to the new god of security—were ready to cast their liberties at its feet without question and dedicate their whole personalities to its being. Many forgot who they were, or where they lived, or what their heritage had been. Forgetting all these things, they seemed to forget that their most sacred rights were theirs inherently rather than doled out by any government or exercised only with the consent of other men. Such capitulation oozed into our democratic institutions. The prevailing, but rarely articulated, assumption seemed to be that liberty was a luxury rather than a source of strength; that security required common agreement on all affairs of state;

that insecurity necessarily would befall any nation whose people criticized their leaders or disagreed about formulation of state policy.

Spontaneous individual support for the nation was treated almost as an unnecessary commodity. Yet history teaches us, or long ago should have taught us, that ultimately national security feeds and thrives upon the strength of individual conviction. Whenever such conviction is shaken, institutions of government tend to reflect the peoples' insecurity by expanding and entrenching their own positions, lending an aura of stability to an inherently unstable condition. At these precise moments in history, basic changes may occur between the people and their government and within the government itself. The post-war years reflect this pattern. The concept of separation of powers was taxed severely. Anyone tutored in, and accustomed to, the behavior of our tripartite government in times of relative security would have good cause for bewilderment.

When the judiciary, by its constitutional mandates, challenged the tendency to deal with heretical thought or apparent heretical action outside the law, or by means which were calculated to slip narrowly within the law, it became the target of criticism from what commonly is referred to as the "left" or "right"—sometimes from both on the same decision. Criticism of the judiciary meant criticism of the judges' decisions and personalities. Judges, of course, are human. They do not wear blinders; they are not made of iron; they are not insensitive. They cannot mount a soapbox in support of unpopular decisions and in the same breath strive to maintain an atmosphere of stilled objectivity. For these very reasons it is of commanding necessity that judges exemplify courage and remain true to their convictions.

I, for one, received a fair amount of correspondence as a result of a decision I felt it necessary to render early in 1955. While I can say, I hope not too immodestly, that most of it was favorable, some of it was not. There were letters and telegrams, some signed, others unsigned. Many of them were prefaced with, "I am not a lawyer, but according to the papers" you subverted this or undermined that. Often the antagonistic letters were addressed fancifully to "U. S. Number One Communist Traitor," or in terms comparably endearing. Probably the most vituperative letter I received was from a retired Brigadier General of the U. S. Army. Many letters proffered hints on how I might improve myself as a judge. You can well imagine my chagrin when, on January 20, 1955, I received the following signed note from a great patriot— a fellow well known to all of you, I am sure. It read:

> "Dear Judge Youngdahl:
> You ought to be impeached, you crook! You are in with the same sneaky, back alley gang that threatens the very life of our great Republic. Don't worry. You'll get yours. The people won't stand for your double-cross.
>
> Very truly yours,
> YANKEE DOODLE JUNIOR"

No amount of abuse, however, can be rationalized into an acceptable excuse for judges becoming spineless and failing to adhere to their personal convictions. Unquestionably, abuse is discouraging. It may even cause depression, but it should never be elevated to a position of such dignity that it can sweep before it principles which give to life its very meaning.

Certainly abuse has not, and never will be, able to inhibit the entire judiciary for very long. In scattered, and at first unpredictable, places during the last few years, the voices of judges and lawyers individually and through associations, rapidly swelled into a ringing demand for a return to sanity —to those sound and tried principles of law as valid in times of insecurity as in times of security. When the judiciary insisted upon adherence to constitutional principles, this natural assumption of authority was viewed as presumptious and with consternation by some in other branches of the government. I think it fair to say that no more than an equality among the three branches of our government was being, and is being, restored. There is no real basis for alarm either by the legislative or the executive branches of the government. The fine balance of separation of powers is being no more than maintained by a delicate and equalizing readjustment.

Accompanying this restoration is a reaffirmation of the truth that national strength rests upon voluntary and spontaneous loyalty. The existence of fair laws fairly executed by reliable institutions nurtures such loyalty. We must now remain vigilant that no one else, private individual or government agency, be permitted to usurp traditional court functions in untried fields, often employing uncommon procedures. Looking back over our history, the major inroads upon individual freedom are traceable to the misuse of legal processes by essentially non-legal institutions. These inroads can be attributed, in part, to the failure to heed the maxim of justice that no man can be trusted as both prosecutor and judge. The executive branch of our government is assigned the mission to investigate crimes and prosecute wrong-doers, among other things. Its task falls short of final adjudication and it must never be permitted to take over this function by bending the courts to its will. Partisan politics or aroused public opinion more easily affect the executive than the courts, resulting in a less healthy forum for the determination of legal rights.

We have suffered a security program where the standards of prohibited conduct were as elusive as the procedure for establishing compliance. The Communist threat was considered a sufficient answer to dispel any criticism. Many abuses were perpetrated, many individuals damaged permanently, and perhaps rendered hesitant to exploit their unqualified right of dissent. As one drop of tainted water in a bucket taints the entire bucket, so in the relatively abstract area of thought and expression one unfounded and arbitrary suppression transcends the individual case and settles upon the thoughts of others like a damper. Our efforts to draw, with exacting precision, a distinction between belief and action must never cease, for only in this way can we keep from orthodoxy, and progress through the resolution of conflicting ideas.

At the same time we must remain wary that the legislative branch of the government does not read too broadly its commission to find facts for prospective legislation. While its broad power to conduct full investigations which look to legislation must be recognized by any sincere proponent of our form of government, such power cannot be, and is not, immeasurable or limitless. When investigations serve no genuine legislative purpose, when they are used primarily for political purposes, when they are used to punish criminal conduct in the absence of evidence and procedure requisite to a similar conviction in a court of law, when they are used to entrap persons into committing some collateral crime such as perjury or contempt, they form no legitimate part of the democratic process as we know it. While the courts may be peculiarly equipped to restrain flagrant misuse of this power, by and large, the real damage flows from the cumulative effect of conduct beyond the legitimate purview of the courts. Final control must ultimately arise from recognition by the legislative branch that investigation is a public trust. Governmental representatives must remain accountable as servants. Moral responsibility must become the handmaiden of authority.

As lawyers, and as members of the judiciary, our task is twofold: First, we must strive to preserve free and searching debate. Using the tools of our trade, we must keep the public better informed as to what limitation may rightfully be imposed upon nonconformity. In this way fear of the unknown is minimized. The area of free discussion, when more clearly delineated, allows all of us to resist more competently intimidation and threats of reprisal where they have no place. We must be mindful of the counsel of Thomas Jefferson who wrote in 1803:

"It behooves every man who values liberty of conscience for himself to resist invasions of it in the case of others."

Second, we must be as watchdogs to see that the laws are kept clear, understandable, and reliable so that the frictions of day-to-day living are minimized and impediments to individual achievement and liberation lessened. I think we can all agree that from an active and satisfied people springs loyalty, and from such loyalty comes national strength. This means that bar associations such as yours carry a heavy responsibility to see that the laws are in fact fairly drawn and impartially executed.

For if there is to be liberty, there must exist an organized society capable of maintaining public order. Blessed with such a society, we face a solemn obligation to draw with fine particularity the boundaries of our liberties.

"I think," said the late Justice Jackson, "that under our system, it is time enough for the law to lay hold of the citizen when he acts illegally, or in some rare circumstances when his thoughts are given illegal utterance. I think we must let his mind alone."

We would do well to heed his observations. Although we recognize the fringe areas of application, we cannot afford to treat thought, speech, and action as less than distinctly unique and separate concepts. We cannot afford to create out of them a new mongrel liberty so broad as to cover everything and so inherently feeble as to protect nothing. If we are to progress, if we are to remain strong and be maintained by an informed citizenry we had best treat speech as more akin to thought, and err, if we must, in favor of inviolate thought. We had best cling tenaciously to our God-given right to think and believe what we will. We should welcome conflicting thought knowing that the search for truth is endless and only through the combat of ideas do we come to recognize error and advance on truth. No man is infallible. No man can be considered the oracle of final truth. The heresies of yesterday often become the acceptable beliefs of today and even the orthodoxies of tomorrow. We may disagree with some heresy, belief, or orthodoxy but no man is entitled to gain acceptance of his ideas through the suppression of another's.

It must follow that we encounter truth only through liberty. We secure liberty only through the courageous application of the best thoughts of watchful men. If this is our promise, so must it be our communal responsibility.

CHAPTER XIV

We've Got to Go Out—
We Don't Have to Come Back

The fighting has officially stopped!

The President of the United States has just declared the cessation of hostilities in the most destructive war of all history. Victory in this war has come to us since the Legislature last assembled. Our young men and women no longer face the horrors of modern war. Thanks be to God, most of them are home again. We who have survived the terrific struggle have a profound obligation to the thousands who did not come back. It is our sacred duty to carry on now with the same steadfastness and devotion which they so unselfishly gave in war. Because of their sacrifice, we are able to meet here today—an assembly of free people. We prove ourselves worthy of their sacrifice only as we consecrate ourselves in the highest degree to the great task of building the peace.

The men, the women, and the children of Minnesota worked long and hard at home, in field, in factory, and in mines to support our fighting men. Because of the efforts of all those who worked and fought and died, the world today has a hope for peace through the United Nations. We pray God that it may succeed!

Aesop, in one of his fables, tells of a lion and a goat quarreling at a water hole as to which should drink first, although there was plenty of room for them to drink together. As they were preparing to fight it out, they looked up and saw some vultures wheeling low above them, waiting for the battle and its aftermath. So, says the fable, they decided to drink together. The vultures fly low over the world today. They have picked the bones of previous civilizations that have fought it out. That shall be our fate, too, unless we learn to live together.

We meet here in this fifty-fifth session of the Legislature during one of the most crucial and difficult periods of American history. In the wake of war are many problems. This first postwar Legislative session presents to us, as the chosen leaders of the people, a heavy burden of responsibility. But it also presents an opportunity for real service by establishing a record of constructive achievement that will be far-reaching in its effect upon future generations in Minnesota. The task will not be easy. In our all-out participation in the war so recently ended, we have had to neglect many services and activities which are vital to the well-being of our state. Now that the fighting has stopped, we must marshal our energies and resources to meet these needs.

Never before in the history of this state has the Legislature faced so many serious needs for our schools, for the mentally ill, and for welfare and other services. These demands confront us at a time when our state income is falling from temporary high war levels. Sky-rocketing costs have aggravated the situation. We know what has happened to our family budgets as a result of the deflated value of the dollar. What affects us in balancing our family budgets affects as well the operations of the state's business. For example, the cost of clothing for those in our mental institutions has risen as much as two and three hundred per cent.

Despite these increased costs, we must meet the impelling needs. Money that is carefully appropriated for our schools, for certain essential activities in home building, for public health, for care for the mentally sick, for dependent children, for the blind, and for the recreation and guidance of our youth, is not an expenditure in the real sense of the word. It is an investment in the character, stability and happiness of our people. I feel confident that the great majority of the people of Minnesota are determined that we shall meet these needs, and that they are willing to pay for them through as fair a method of taxation as can be devised.

The war caused many strains and disruptions of our economy. We in government and industry are busy reconverting our economy of war into one of peace. In business and finance, we quickly see the need for this economic reconversion. But we are not always so ready to see the importance of bolstering our moral and spiritual resources, which, in the disillusioning aftermath of war, suffer a slump. We must have the vision to encourage those activities which build up the decencies of human life — the spiritual qualities that redeem man from brutality and give him moral dignity and worth.

General Douglas MacArthur, as he accepted the surrender of the Japanese militarists on the battleship "Missouri," pointed to the basic need of the world. He said that we required a moral regeneration—that it must be of the spirit if we are to save the flesh. Yes, men are redeemed spiritually through the still, small voice of conscience, properly disciplined by the teachings of home, church and school.

Therefore, let us resolve to strengthen these institutions. We have advanced far in penetrating the frontiers of science. The frontier of the next few decades which we must explore is that of the field of human relations. There is no alternative if the world is to survive. And we must begin right here in our state—Minnesota—and in our home communities and families.

We have long talked about World Brotherhood. It was a beautiful ideal. Today, it is no longer an ideal, but an absolute necessity. The fate of civilization hangs in balance. We must have World Brotherhood, or else! The war has brought home to us the grim picture of what that "or else" means. The thousands upon thousands of starving Greeks; the hollow-cheeked Frenchmen eating thistles; the terrible slaughter of the Polish Jews; the children of undernourished mothers being born, literally, without fingernails; the torture of Norwegians in concentration camps; the death march at Bataan; the merciless beheading of our own airmen—these fill the pages of the history of World War II. We ought to know by now that we must have brotherhood, or else. We will secure brotherhood by building up our human resources at the community level. It will cost money. But there is no alternative. We have got to find the way.

It is related that off the New England Coast a ship was hurled mercilessly against the rocks. The Coast Guard arrived, under the command of an experienced captain. There were some inexperienced fellows on board who lacked vision and courage. One of them said to the captain, "Captain, with that tide against us and the terrific gale, we will be able to get out there all right, but we will never be able to get back." To this the captain responded, "Prepare the boat. We have to go out; we don't have to come back."

And so it is with us. Despite the difficulties, we have got to find the means to conduct research in the field of human engineering. If we did not shirk in financing a war, bringing unfathomable destruction, we dare not shirk the much lighter task of financing construction. We have got to go out; we don't have to come back. Who wants to come back to Hiroshima? Who wants to come back to Nagasaki? Who wants to come back to a world on fire?

Through education and all the moral and spiritual forces at our command we must take up the continual battle against the evils of greed, bigotry and war. The future depends upon whether we learn the simple but seemingly difficult lesson of living together in a spirit of understanding and amity, regardless of differences of color, creed, political or religious convictions, or circumstances of birth. Like the animals in Aesop's fable, either we must live together, or we shall perish.

Four broad but impelling objectives urge us to joint action at this historic session of the Legislature.

I. We must build up our human resources.

II. We must strengthen our economic resources.

III. We must increase the efficiency of our state government.

IV. Boldly, we must provide the necessary revenue to meet our challenging post-war needs.

I. THE FIRST OBJECTIVE: EDUCATION

In the attainment of our first objective, which is to strengthen our human resources, our school system will play a vital part. UNESCO, the United Nations' Educational, Scientific and Cultural Organization, one of the most important agencies of the United Nations, is meeting in an historic session at the very time when we meet to strengthen the educational standards of our state. Here are the first words of UNESCO's constitution: "Since wars begin in the minds of men, it is in the minds of men that defenses of peace must be constructed." Peace begins on our own street. It begins in our homes; in our churches; in our schools. Strengthen these institutions and we improve our chances for peace. Education must now be given its full day in court. We must do our part here in Minnesota. Although the last Legislature appropriated more for state aid than at any other time, we face an impelling need for more aid for the common schools.

* * * * *

Minnesota ranks very poorly when compared with other states in the number of farm boys who graduate from high school. This is unfair to our rural youth; it is also unfair to our state. Our history sparkles with stories of farm boys who have become state and national leaders. Even though they choose agriculture as their career — and there is no more worthy vocation—they should have the benefit of at least a high school education to keep pace with an industry that is becoming increasingly scientific.

* * * * *

During recent years the operation of our schools has been handicapped by a shortage of qualified teachers which, in turn, has been caused by inadequate salaries. Therefore, in addition to the State Aid Bill, I recommend that we further advance our educational system by the passage of a minimum teachers' salary law, making compliance with it a condition of receiving state aid. I would suggest not less than the minimum schedule of salaries as approved by the Minnesota Educational Association.

Our supply of trained teachers would be further increased by the establishment of scholarships by which young people would be encouraged to enter the teaching profession. The selection of candidates could well be made by a committee from the state Department of Education and the teachers' colleges. Any student receiving such a scholarship would agree to teach in the elementary schools of the state for one year for each year's scholarship grant, or repay the grant.

* * * * *

Directly related to aid for the common schools is the need for further support of our teachers' colleges. More money will be required for equipment, increased salaries and better services if we are to succeed in encouraging more of our young men and women to become teachers. I recommend, also, the establishment of the position of an administrative head under the teachers' college board to integrate the activities of all teachers' colleges.

* * * * *

More than 27,300 students are now enrolled at our great State University, the greatest enrollment in its history. Staffs, salaries, space and equipment are plainly inadequate in the face of this unprecedented problem. The Federal Government, through payment of special tuitions to war veterans, has increased its aid to the University, and the state must do its share in providing financial assistance. Our institutions of higher learning carry on valuable research that continually penetrates new frontiers of science. The value of this research was made outstandingly clear during the war. We must do all we can to enable Minnesota institutions to carry on in research and in the training of future scientists.

We have considered our educational system, and some of the means by which it may be improved. Some may say that we cannot afford these improvements; that we have reached the limit of our appropriations. I submit this proposition: we cannot afford *not* to invest more money in education. If education is to be rescued from its present peril, we have no alternative. Courageously, in spite of all difficulties, we must launch out!

* * * * *

HOUSING

Perhaps no matter is more constantly before us these days than the housing shortage. This is not simply a problem of lumber and bricks, but is directly related to our first main objective, the conservation of human resources. Worry, broken homes, juvenile delinquency—these are but a few of the evils which follow in the train of the housing shortage. To say that our Federal Government has bungled the job of providing homes may well be true, but naming a scapegoat will not supply more homes for anyone. In the interest of veterans and all citizens who deserve and demand decent housing, we must meet the emergency by matching Federal aid with state action.

The state and its communities, in cooperation with private industry and the agencies of the Federal Government, must do everything possible to provide temporary housing until the snarls in the construction of housing can be untangled. Another way in which the state can assist is through the mobilization of its natural resources, and through encouragement of increased production of building materials within our own state.

For the coordination of all housing activities in the state, including research, I recommend the establishment of a Housing Commission. The staff should consist of an executive secretary who should be an expert in the housing field, with such advisory members on a non-compensated basis as would represent all groups interested in the problem.

* * * * *

Minnesota is one of the very few states which has failed to provide enabling legislation by which those local public bodies wishing to do so, can obtain Federal funds made available for housing programs. The Legislature should provide such a law at this session.

* * * * *

It is also necessary to give consideration to more desirable methods than now provided by law for urban redevelopment of slum areas. The present law has been ineffective. Since it should be our policy that effective housing programs must operate within the framework of local government and planning, the responsibility for urban development plans rests on the local communities. However, the state should permit such undertakings as are consistent with the overall policy of the state. A number of plans have been in operation in other states for clearing and redeveloping blighted areas, and there will be put before you a bill embodying the best features of these plans that will conform to present and contemplated Federal legislation. I hope you may see fit to have such a law here.

* * * * *

You should also consider legislation which will protect relief clients under long term leases.

MENTAL HOSPITALS

We have stated our first objective to be the conservation of our human resources. Another aspect of this main objective is support for our mental hospitals.

Minnesota is below the average among the states in the care of the mentally ill. We should not be satisfied until we have done everything possible to assist the unfortunate individuals confined in these institutions, and to re-establish as many of them as possible as useful members of society. Consideration should be given to providing adequate psychiatric service for each mental hospital.

* * * * *

One of the more urgently needed improvements in our program for the mentally ill is an institution for children with serious mental and emotional disturbances who are unable to adjust themselves either in their own homes or in foster homes, and for whom no facilities are available at the present time. It is recommended that the Legislature authorize as a part of the appropriation for mental hospitals the construction and operation of such a children's institution, and until a building can be provided, temporary facilities should be established for this purpose.

* * * * *

The minimum requirements for our mental institutions will be presented to you in my budget message.

* * * * *

SOCIAL WELFARE

Turning to another phase of our human resources, we consider our services in social welfare, our aid to the aged, to dependent children, and to the blind.

The present Old Age Assistance Law places a limit of forty dollars per month on the amount which a person may receive for the necessities of life, exclusive of medical care. Many recipients of old age assistance cannot maintain a standard of living on this amount compatible with health and decency. Therefore, the present maximum should either be raised or eliminated. If a maximum is retained, the Act should be amended to permit county welfare boards to grant supplemental assistance from county funds in special hardship cases.

It is equally obvious that the present maxima in the program for aid to dependent children are too low. These maxima should also be generously increased or removed entirely so that mothers who have dependent children can rear them properly in their own homes and provide them with the necessities of life.

Minnesota's child-care program is based on the idea that a family group is the best setting in which to rear a normal child, and long strides have been made in recent years toward caring for children in foster homes under the state's guardianship. The Legislature should provide adequate funds, and every effort should be made both administratively and by law to perfect this splendid type of child care.

* * * * *

Similarly, the blind are entitled to certain liberalizing amendments in the laws enacted on their behalf.

* * * * *

PUBLIC HEALTH

Still another aspect of our first objective is the conservation of public health. The key person in our public health program is the county nurse. Upon her is placed a great number and variety of important duties, including maternity and orthopedic service, venereal disease and tuberculosis control. She assists in all phases of community health. And yet there are many counties in the state which do not presently have a public health nurse.

I recommend that legislation be passed to provide partial financial support for every county which hires a public health nurse.

The budget message will recommend, in addition, an expansion of the school dental health program, designed to educate children in the proper care of their teeth.

The industrial public health program should be continued, since it can be of particular value in improving health standards in small business.

Another step that should be considered is the passage of enabling legislation permitting the establishment of county and district health departments.

* * * * *

YOUTH CONSERVATION

We come now to a problem which, as you know, is of special interest to me—the conservation of our youth. Here is one of our greatest human resources. The time has come when we must reappraise our whole philosophy in connection with the problems of youth. It deserves our special consideration and prompt action. It is essentially a problem of prevention. The factors which have caused juvenile delinquency are multiple and complex and our attack must likewise be many-sided. Every institution and agency must be used: homes, churches, schools, recreational centers, health services, child guidance clinics, and every interested public and private group.

* * * * *

There will be submitted for your consideration a Youth Conservation Act. By this legislation we will promote good citizenship, attack the problem of delinquency and, if all else fails and a youthful offender is brought into court, we will provide appropriate treatment for each specific case.

* * * * *

This matter of youth conservation, although somewhat intangible, is desperately real. We must face it; we must attack it; we have got to launch out.

* * * * *

LAW ENFORCEMENT

To implement our constructive program for the strengthening of those great human resources which are to be found in the youth of our state, it is my intention to do everything in my power to enforce the laws of this state fairly, fearlessly and effectively.

* * * * *

I favor a strengthening of the provisions and enforcement of laws relating to the sale and licensing of beer and intoxicating liquors. There should be uniform standards for licensing, uniform closing hours, and uniform regulations with respect to the presence of minors.

I further favor a law which would forfeit any license (liquor, food or any other license) of any business establishment in which slot machines or any other gambling devices are maintained and operated.

I believe, also, that a law should be passed making it illegal to use the telegraph, telephone or other means of communication for transmitting bets or wagers or information regarding betting, wagering or any other illegal transaction.

* * * * *

HUMAN RELATIONS

As the final aspect of our first main objective, we come to the important problem of promoting good will between racial and religious groups. In the great arena of international relationships, we are all deeply concerned. Regardless of differences in ideology, we are concerned with the problem of getting along with Russia; we are concerned with the relations between colonial powers and their colonies; we are concerned with the development of friendship between Orientals and Occidentals; we are concerned that all men should learn to live together as brothers.

Essentially this is a matter of conscience and good will; living together cannot be accomplished legislatively, but to prevent injustice, legislation is necessary. It should provide every opportunity through investigation and conciliation to eliminate discrimination. As a last resort any person who has suffered from discrimination and who has exhausted all the possibilities of conciliation should have legal recourse in the courts of the state. Elaborate administrative machinery is not necessary. One full-time official, assisted by the advisory group of the Inter-Racial Commission, would be able to administer such a law. We would thus make a specific contribution toward the building of a society with equal opportunity for all its citizens.

I have discussed at some length the conservation of our human resources. These are the greatest assets of our state. An enlightened citizenry, showing a concern for its handicapped and needy members, courageously attacking the problems of education, housing, public health, youth conservation and racial discrimination—here is a goal that is worthy of all the thought and energy at our command, and if the faint heart should object that the difficulties lying in our course are insuperable, our answer must be, "We have no alternative; we have got to launch out!"

* * * * *

II. ECONOMIC RESOURCES CONSERVATION

We come now to our second main objective, the conservation and growth of our economic resources. Minnesota has been fortunately endowed with a great wealth of forests, lakes, streams and minerals. We are the custodians of that wealth. I know that you concur with me in wanting to see an active campaign of conservation of these resources that will move forward on all fronts in this postwar period.

Such legislation as is necessary should be enacted for the continuance and expansion of a broad and comprehensive conservation program, including effective soil conservation; improvement of public waters and elimination of pollution; forestry development; adequate fire control; provisions for selective cutting and timber management; an aggressive program of propagating and improving game and fish resources and removal of rough fish; promotion of the tourist industry; further development of the use of the state's parks, and a long-range program for balanced mining of low-grade and high-grade iron ore to prolong the life of mining in Minnesota.

* * * * *

MANAGEMENT-LABOR RELATIONS

Another way of strengthening our economic resources is to maintain stability in management-labor relations. Minnesota has had an enviable record under its labor-relations law. I believe that law should be continued and that we should be cautious in changing it unless we are sure that amendments will improve its operation and make for greater stability.

I do not believe that stability will be achieved by punitive methods against labor. I do not believe that the great mass of employers want to see restrictive methods used against our workers, nor do I believe that the rank and file of working men and women want to see unfair methods used against employers. Both groups, in the main, prefer to adjust their differences peacefully — through negotiation rather than through conflict—and we should continue to keep the emphasis on conciliation, with a minimum of restriction.

* * * * *

AGRICULTURE

Agriculture is another vital economic resource of the state. The prosperity of us all, either directly or indirectly, is dependent upon the well-being of the thousands of farms that stretch from one end of this state to the other.

Problems of agriculture transcend lines of state authority for the most part and only the Federal Government is in a position to deal effectively with many of them. The state can, however, take action in certain areas.

If we provide adequate financial resources, our farm schools and agricultural scientists can keep a steady march forward in developing new crops, better livestock, better soil conservation practices and better methods of weed eradication. We must encourage the processing of our farm products right here in Minnesota and be vigorous in promoting expanded markets. We should encourage the constructive work being accomplished by the 4-H Clubs and the Future Farmers of America in our rural communities.

* * * * *

III. GOVERNMENTAL EFFICIENCY REORGANIZATION

Let us now turn our attention to the third objective— that of increasing the efficiency, economy and sound operation of our state government. I believe that now is a good time to consider the matter of further improvement in the reorganization of our state government. I commend you for your announced purpose of simplifying legislative procedure. In the Executive branch a wonderful start was made in 1939 with the civil service system, the addition of a business manager plan which has established a national reputation, and other modern improvements in governmental machinery. I believe that these improvements should be continued and strengthened and that attempts at further reorganization should be made. I hope to confer and work with the Committees on Civil Administration on the matter of further improvements and reorganization.

* * * * *

LEGISLATIVE RESEARCH COUNCIL

In order to further improve the legislative machinery of our government, I recommend the establishment of a Legislative Research Council. A Legislative Research Council should consist of an outstanding research director, a small staff, and such members of the legislature as you may determine. The Council would not have power to initiate legislation or determine policy, but would be primarily concerned with making impartial studies of important problems and securing all the essential facts. This would promote sound legislation. There was a time when the Legislature could discharge its duties in a short biennial session. Today, however, state government, to be effective, must be a continuous process. Because our Legislature lacks some of the modern tools of government, controversial and important legislation frequently must be enacted with undue haste. Or, because of lack of factual data, currently pressing problems have to be postponed until the next session.

A third factor which militates against constructive legislation is the fact that selfish pressure groups, loud in their protestations, seek to secure legislation for their own interests, and to obstruct legislation if it does not serve their interests. The Legislative Research Council will help neutralize these pressure groups. As legislators you deserve the best in tested and scientific instruments. Only through the ascertainment of impartial data can the Legislature act with a minimum of misunderstanding, controversy and delay.

* * * * *

IV. NEW REVENUE

We come now to the fourth and final objective, namely, to boldly provide the necessary revenue to meet our challenging postwar needs.

* * * * *

In addition to the cost of operating our state departments, as will be suggested in the budget message to be given you

in a few days, I have pointed out in this message some of
the expanding needs of the next biennium. It would not be
fair for me to suggest these needs without at least pointing
out what I think the fairest approach should be in raising
the new revenue. But before discussing methods of raising
new revenue, I would like to stress the importance of
economy in our state government. Not a dollar of the state's
money should be spent without the closest scrutiny. In the face
of the tremendous needs, we should be especially vigilant to
see to it that full value is received in the expenditure of
state funds.

I do not believe that a general sales tax is the fairest type
of tax because it tends to place a relatively heavier burden
on the man of small income than on the man of large income.
Nor do I believe that taxes on real property should be increased except as a last resort.

I have made a careful study of all the possibilities for
additional revenue and have concluded that the fairest
approach that can be made to the problem would be to provide additional revenue on certain luxury items. The official
declaration of the end of hostilities will automatically
eliminate some luxury items in the Federal area of taxation
on July first. This will open the way in the luxury field for
new taxes at the state level. Doubling the present liquor
tax rate would yield about six or seven million dollars additional revenue per year. A two-cent cigarette tax would return between three and one-half and four million dollars
per year, with an additional $400,000 per year if all tobacco
products were taxed. A three-cent cigarette tax would return
in tax receipts between five and one-half and six million
dollars per year, with an additional $600,000 per year if all
tobacco products were taxed. An admissions tax of twenty

per cent, assuming that the same pattern of spending for 1947 as for 1946 is followed, would result in an estimated revenue of from five million to five and one-half million dollars per year. A cabaret or night club tax of thirty per cent, assuming no change in the spending pattern in 1947 as compared with 1946, would bring estimated tax receipts of approximately one million dollars per year.

I think, also, consideration should be given by you to the possibility of securing additional revenue from occupational and royalty taxes of iron ore and from gross earnings of utilities and railroads. Of course, it is necessary to consider the tax program which is most sound and constructive from the standpoint of assuring steady jobs and thriving industry. We must constantly analyze our tax structure and insure that it be one which will not cripple the state in the creation of jobs, in the attraction and holding of new industry, and in the wisest development of our natural resources.

Further, I believe there is considerable need for assessment reform. A county supervisor of assessments could be the means of bringing in thousands of dollars of additional revenue by fairer and more adequate assessment of property. With the increased revenue that can be secured from the sources I have suggested, I believe that our budget can be balanced and that we will be able to meet the challenge in providing the basic needs of this postwar period.

The basic problem before you, in seeking these additional funds, will, of course, be the needs of the state. But I want to urge that you give consideration to the plight of local governments. Rising costs have made it difficult for many local units of government, restricted largely to property tax revenue, to finance themselves and maintain the usual services. Local governments are subsidiaries of the state. Unless some answer is found for their urgent financial difficulties, the general welfare of the entire state will be affected. It is up to us to work together in a spirit of harmony and mutual cooperation to work out these difficult financial problems which vitally affect us all.

I believe that enabling legislation, not in conflict with the state's revenue laws, should be passed to permit municipalities to raise additional revenue to help finance their services. I suggest also that you consider the advisability of distributing some part of the new special taxes proposed back to the municipalities to assist them in their difficult financial situation.

Raising new revenues is never a popular or an easy task, but keeping in mind the imperative nature of the needs for which the money is to be raised, we simply have no alternative. We have got to launch out.

* * * * *

I have appreciated the opportunity to talk to many of you Legislators individually concerning these important problems. I have not been able to talk to all of you. I shall welcome the opportunity during the session to consult with any member, regardless of party affiliation, on any problem that concerns the welfare of the state. Our Constitution makes clear the division of powers between the Legislative and Executive branches of government. I want you to know at the outset of our relationship that I shall always be cognizant of that separation of authority. Together, we shall work out a program that will best meet the needs of all the people. Accomplishment can only come through cooperation and hard work by all of us.

Although I believe in the two-party system of government, the governor is elected to serve *all* the people. I shall endeavor to serve you without reference to blocs or pressure groups and without regard to political consequences; I shall attempt to follow my own convictions on any matter that comes before me. I assure you that I am free to do just that. I enter upon my duties in all humility and fully cognizant of my profound obligations.

We shall be facing trying days. The type of world in which we may live for the next quarter or half of a century may well be patterned by the type of thinking and example of our leaders during the next important years. I have sensed among you an appreciation of that fact as I have discussed the problems with you. I can assure you that I am deeply sensitive to it. I would feel very insecure were it not for my faith in God, and the fact that I shall be able to rely upon Him for guidance and support when discouragement and uncertainty come. I pledge to you and the people of this great state my best efforts. I shall consecrate and dedicate myself to serve all the people fairly. Let us, with God's help, join hands to make this a truly historic session in the preservation, conservation and improvement of our economic and human resources.

Over the grave of an American Colonel in Italy, who fell in battle, a Chaplain put as epitaph words that had been familiar on the Colonel's lips, "Always take the high ground and the enemy will flee." If we take the high ground of consecration to public service, no situation can discourage and no disappointment defeat us in reaching our goal.

Today, no less than in war time, there is a premium on fortitude. In the face of tides of apathy, pessimism and timidity, endangered by the jagged rocks of practical difficulties and amid the crosswinds of selfish interests, our duty is still clear. The words of the New England Coast Guard Captain still ring true, and they are spoken to us: "We have got to go out; we don't have to come back."

CHAPTER XV

My Greatest Painting—the Next One

This is 1949, the great Centennial year of Minnesota.

A great painter whose hand produced many a work of art was asked, "Which is your greatest painting?" The artist paused a moment. "My greatest painting? The next one!"

The people of our state, in this Centennial year, look back upon a record of achievement. 1849-1949, a century of struggle and growth, a century of toil and sacrifice, a century in which a wilderness has been transformed into a great, progressive commonwealth. The Centennial year marks a luminous place along our path; a year dedicated to the people who built Minnesota, to the countless unnamed pioneers who believed enough in her future to be pioneers; to the laborers in our iron mines or in the foundries of our cities; to the tillers of the soil who cleared a wilderness and brought out of it rich farms; to the vision of countless merchants and businessmen on our thousands of main streets; to the courage of the leaders of industry who launched out to new frontiers; to the men of the various professions who helped and guided and counseled their fellowmen; to the homemakers, the teachers, the political leaders, the religious leaders—to all who have built homes, schools, churches, and better communities—to all these we pay our tribute. All these were the builders of Minnesota.

The temptation at any anniversary observance is to glorify the past at the expense of the future. We honor the past; without it there would be no great present, but our eyes are fixed upon the future. The people of Minnesota, like the famous painter, are being asked to name their greatest century. Their reply must be, "The next one!"

This next century depends upon the way in which we, the descendants of these great pioneers, build for the future; the way in which we, the children of those sturdy people, maintain the security, the freedom, and the democracy which we have inherited from them.

Two years ago the fighting had just officially stopped. We then faced a great challenge; we met in a critical hour of history. Today the problems are more complex and the challenge greater than ever.

Not so long ago a group of miners were entombed in one of the Kimberly Diamond Mines in South Africa. Surrounded by unlimited riches, they slowly met their death. Starving for food, thirsting for water, in need of medical assistance, deprived of spiritual comfort, diamonds were worthless.

And so it is in our world today. We are discovering that accepted values must be reappraised. We are coming to understand that our claim to distinction and progress has been based on false standards.

We have been worshipping the gods of science and material advancement until now we see ourselves trapped by the monstrous weapons we have devised. Our ability to create has surpassed our ability to utilize wisely the products of our invention.

We are learned in the art of war—we are ignorant in the art of peace. We are proficient in the art of killing—we are unskilled in the art of living. We probe and grasp the mystery of atomic fission—we reject the Golden Rule and the Sermon on the Mount. We are being entombed to our death in the diamond mine of materialism.

There must be a place in our scheme of things for those great intangible human values which cannot be represented on graphs or ledgers. Our values must stem from the Fatherhood of God and the Brotherhood of man. We must stop gauging our success by production of machines or dollars of income. We have got to understand that important as it is to produce efficiency in the factory, it is even more important to build character in its workers and to turn out a product that will strengthen our nation. No standard of living is high when jobs become drudgery and hours dreary; when rancor and bitterness exist between management and labor; when young men and women can't afford a family; when children in slums are walled off by brick from sod and sky; where there is not equality of educational opportunity for every boy and girl; where decent health conditions are not afforded to all of our people. No standard of living is high where we do not fulfill our obligation to the needy, the aged, the crippled, the blind, the dependent and neglected children; where we fail in our duty to the individual sick of mind; when we deny equal rights to our people because of race, creed, color, or nationality.

As we face the new century in Minnesota history we are confronted by a two-fold task: first, to mark out new horizons in human goals for which we strive; second, to provide economic means by which these goals may be achieved.

I. *THE GOALS FOR WHICH WE STRIVE*

1. MENTAL HEALTH

First in the consideration of our human goals is the mental health of our people. There are more than 10,500 individuals of good soul but sick mind in our state mental hospitals. They are but the vanguard of a vast number to follow, in which—and mark this well!—will be represented one member out of every five families. Unless modern research and preventive measures are immediately introduced, a large percentage of these people will continue to constitute a major human resource rushing down the drainpipe of social neglect.

Most persons have accepted without much questioning the idea, so widely prevalent, that there is some stigma attached to mental illness, that nothing can be done about it and that the unhappy victims must be put away somewhere in an institution to spend the rest of their days. These ridiculed, abused, and maligned members of our social family cannot speak for themselves. They are made mute by sickness, guarded walls, and the loss of their civil rights. Their heartbroken families are rendered equally silent by the cruel stigma which false social attitudes attach to the mentally ill. Casualties of the spirit, voiceless and powerless, their personalities—yes, their very lives—are completely dependent on the concern, wisdom, and compassion of those of us who are more fortunate.

We need not detail here the disclosures of conditions which have shocked those of us who have visited our mental hospitals here in Minnesota; the rows upon rows of unattended human beings, regimented and neglected because of lack of help, living lives of grim monotony and deteriorating emptiness, deprived of human rights and necessities.

In other states, conditions are much the same. Nowhere is man's inhumanity to man more pronounced than in our care of the mentally ill.

The mental hospital of today is only a superstructure built on the foundation of the old asylum, representing a social monstrosity which plagues the whole nation with shame and disgrace. It fails to return to society that high percentage of patients for whom modern psychiatry holds out hope. It similarly denies the milk of human kindness to those patients who, under present levels of scientific knowledge, are incurable. I caution here against any consideration of this problem which confines its attention solely to those deemed curable; even the most hopeless patient in our hospitals has something so precious that it cannot be judged in values other than human and divine.

The mental hospital system is the only major American social institution which has remained fundamentally unchanged since the abolition of its moral counterpart, slavery.

Our system of caring for and treating these sick human beings is outmoded. To protect society from the so-called "dangerous," to confine the helpless, to furnish a roof to house those falsely thought to be incurable—for this we would need only brick and mortar. We would need only fortified buildings to lock the patients in and the public out.

* * * * *

But the time when the mentally ill could be put away in an institution, "out of sight—out of mind," must end. I propose that we inaugurate the Centennial year by pioneering to make the mental hospital in Minnesota a house of hope, rather than a habitation for the living dead. I propose that we equip our mental hospitals to give our patients the best possible care and extend to those who can be cured the fullest opportunity for rehabilitation. Many of the mentally ill in our hospitals can be restored to health with proper treatment, we now know, and go home to live normal, useful lives.

Our human goal should be to make Minnesota the first state in the nation to reach the standards of decency as are reflected by the standards of the American Psychiatric Association.

You have in previous sessions shown your sympathies by generous appropriations for the type of system which has prevailed. At the last session you approved a comprehensive and progressive building program, much of which is now under way. This session, I trust, will take the decisive step to adopt a new approach for the care of the mentally ill. The modern therapeutic center, "the house of hope," would replace the traditional state hospital. Characterized by research and active training of personnel, it would have links with the home and community through clinics and social work services, which would in turn provide early detection, possible non-hospital treatment, post-hospital follow-up care of discharged patients, and consultative and other services to courts, schools, and welfare agencies.

The details of this program will be supplied in my budgetary message. It is based not on how cheaply we can maintain a patient for life, but on how early we can detect his illness, how actively we can treat it, and how quickly we can discharge him. It is intended to increase the number of citizens returning to enrich the lives of their communities. In time it would end the costly and vicious circle of building an ever-expanding system of costly custodial buildings to house an ever-increasing backlog of needlessly deteriorating patients.

* * * * *

Due to low quotas, low salaries, lack of training, and shortages of trained personnel, we have a psychiatric corps large enough to serve less than 4,000 of the 10,500 patients in our seven mental hospitals. The situation in the institutions for the mentally deficient and epileptic is similar. Without trained personnel, physical facilities are of no avail.

Therefore, I recommend that we establish a quota of psychiatric workers in our mental health system which would permit us to reach the standards of the American Psychiatric Association during this biennium.

How will we obtain this personnel? First, we must go out into the open market and offer competitive salaries; second, we must train people to fill vacancies. The budget message will contain provisions to establish in the state hospitals at Hastings and Rochester the first two units of a proposed teaching service for the state, for the training of doctors and other members of the psychiatric team in short supply. Third, we must establish the 40-hour work week. Fourth, we must provide adequate housing for all employees living on the grounds.

One of the most vital posts in the psychiatric team is now held by the position, which since asylum days, has been termed "attendant." The term and function of "attendant" must be changed. The psychiatric worker for this position should be more than a mere guard and housekeeper. After additional scientific training he would be eligible for more specialized and responsible tasks.

One of the major and most justifiable criticisms against American mental hospitals pertains to the vicious caste system, typified by the double standard of diet. Unless we end the double standard of diet, we cannot expect that patients will have the feeling that the institution exists for them and not they for the institution. As a necessary step to increase the recovery rate—as a factor even more important than mere nutrition—the program recommends funds, equipment, and dietitians to assure every patient a decent standard of food at least equal to that of the employees.

The program calls for adequate support of occupational, recreational, and other therapies designed to end the deteriorating idleness of state hospitals. The program calls for improved living conditions, adequate clothing, linens, and other personal necessities. Certain features deal with accelerated control of tuberculosis and other communicable diseases. The death rate from tuberculosis in our institutions is twenty times that of our general population. The program also would provide for an adequate staff of chaplains to give spiritual help and counsel to the patients.

Social systems, particularly those deeply rooted in the superstitions of our asylum past, are not changed over night. The program constitutes only the bare minimum required to start us on the long road ahead. It calls only for those factors which can be absorbed administratively in the next biennium. Due to the inflationary costs of building today, as well as to the increased expenses of introducing this pioneering service, requests for capital expansion and equipment, except where vitally necessary or to complete the current building program, will be deferred.

I also recommend (1) changes in the archaic terminology and content in laws relating to mental illness, and (2) statutory provisions for transfer of the mental health authority from the Department of Health to a separate bureau in the Division of Public Institutions, in which would be organized all mental health activities.

* * * * *

Human misery knows no geographical borders. We cannot hide behind the fact that conditions in other states are comparable to ours. We cannot hide behind the fact that no one individual is solely responsible for our "snake pits" and "bedlams." *Particeps criminis*. We have all participated in a social crime. Listen to the words of a grand jury investigating similar conditions in a mental hospital in another state:

"The grand jury condemns the whole system that today allows this unholy thing to exist in our state. The responsibility is widespread and it must be met. All must share in the guilt for this social crime against these innocent and helpless people. All must share in the responsibility for instituting redress of this long-standing and terrible injustice."

The advance we are proposing in the frontier of mental health is the first and one of the most crucial of our human goals. Our mental hospitals may be no worse than the national average. But we must remember this: salvation comes to human society through vigorous minorities keeping alive a zealous protest against the deification of the average. The average is not good enough. We must not rest until Minnesota achieves the pre-eminent place among the states of the nation in its ministration to those who are mentally ill.

2. EDUCATION

The second important human goal is education. One hundred years ago Horace Mann, one of the great pioneers in education, affirmed that the aspirations for and the faith in the future of the human race ". . . depend upon teachers, more than upon *any*, more than upon *all* other human instrumentalities united." Almost a century later James Hilton also expressed the significance of the teacher in our society when he said: "If I had a child who wanted to be a teacher I would give him Godspeed as if he were going to a war. For indeed the war against prejudice, greed and ignorance is eternal, and those who dedicate themselves to it give their lives no less because they may live to see some fraction of the battle won. They are the commandoes of the place, if peace is to be more than a short armistice. As in a relay race, our armed men have handed victory to those who dare not stand still to admire it, but must run with it for very life to a further and larger goal."

We have come a long way in education in this past century, but there is still much to be done. Education has lagged behind our material progress. In the next century we must stress social, civic, moral, and spiritual literacy more than the accumulation of facts and a shrewd canniness of the intellect.

In your last session you made a significant advance in the improvement of education and the people of the state have given admirable cooperation to the program.

The cost of education has increased in recent years, the enrollments have been enlarged, and there is a pressing demand for additional services. These factors require substantially greater funds to achieve this human goal. Blessed by recent years of unparalleled prosperity, we must not fail our youth.

* * * * *

We must meet the necessity of sound preparation, adequate compensation, and retirement protection for teachers. I am of the opinion that we are already past the time when anything less than two years' preparation should be accepted for a certificate to teach in the schools of Minnesota, and that as soon as possible the requirement should be raised above that level. I still believe the law should establish minimum salary regulations below which no teacher can be employed.

During recent years we have been confronted with the grave problem of an inadequate supply of well-trained teachers. I believe that one way in which the state can help would be by making available scholarships to provide partial financial assistance to capable young men and women wishing to take college courses that will prepare them for teaching careers. The student receiving such a scholarship would fulfill his part of the bargain by agreeing to teach in the elementary schools of the state for one year for each year's scholarship grant, or else he would repay the grant received.

An adequate supply of well-prepared teachers depends directly upon equipping, staffing, and financing the institutions in which our teachers are educated. This includes the teachers' colleges and a portion of the University. It is of prime importance that the facilities of these institutions for teachers' education be substantially financed. I recommend a careful study of the salary schedule for the faculty of the teachers' colleges to determine what adjustments are necessary. It is likewise vital to the educational, scientific, and cultural development of our state that the whole enterprise of higher education be given wholehearted support both morally and financially. Besides the need for operating funds, there are staggering needs for building, which deserve your serious consideration and support.

* * * * *

The funds we appropriate to achieve our second human goal should be regarded as investments rather than expenditures. A sound education is one of the essentials for a strong democracy.

3. YOUTH CONSERVATION

The third of the great human goals for which we strive is the conservation of our youth.

A farmer was shown a gnarled and twisted tree, and was asked his opinion as to the cause of its distortion. His answer was, "Someone must have stepped on it when it was young." In Minnesota we place prime value on our boys and girls, our young men and young women. We are determined that they shall not be "stepped on" by an unthinking and unfeeling society. You gave tangible expression to the people's determination by your enactment of our Youth Conservation Act. The operation of this measure insures that we handle the lives of our youth as human personalities and not as depersonalized problem cases. The soul of the most reprobate child is fully worthy of salvation.

The Commission, though it has been handicapped by a lack of funds, has impressive accomplishments to its credit. We must strengthen its hands. As you know, we have had to use our present institutions for diagnostic centers. This is not an ideal situation. While the institutions have cooperated fully in helping to create and maintain these centers, the necessity of having a youth placed within an institution has brought about difficulties of administration. It has also tended to some degree to label children and youths who were held in the reception center as inmates of the institutions of which they were a part.

* * * * *

To more effectively develop this diagnostic program for our youth, I believe we should establish a Youth Conservation Reception Center in the vicinity of the Twin Cities where we can get the benefit of professional assistance at the University of Minnesota.

4. SOCIAL WELFARE

We proceed to a discussion of our fourth human goal, Social Welfare.

Today our welfare program ranks foremost in the country. But we must not stand still. We must continue to search for improvement.

For example, considerable success has been achieved in the placement of dependent children in permanent homes under existing legislation. In fact, our state has attracted national attention for its efforts to find homes for both the normal child and the child with handicaps. We are now at a point where this service could be improved by amending the law to permit welfare boards with adequate facilities and staffs to place children for adoption. The purpose of this is to speed up the finding of homes for dependent children on public support, many of whom in the past have been considered unplaceable.

* * * * *

Now, with respect to the public assistance grants, our present Old Age Assistance Law establishes a $50 maximum upon any individual grant, except for medical care. In giving aid to dependent children, the maximum grant is $50 for a mother and one child, $20 for the second child, and $15 for each additional child. In the latter program, there is no special provision for medical care. In addition, local jurisdictions may supplement these payments from their own relief funds. I favor a much more workable system of granting assistance strictly in accordance with the needs of each individual.

Therefore, I recommend to this Legislature that it remove the maxima in old age assistance and aid to dependent children and provide, instead, that assistance be granted in accordance with the need determined to exist in each case. The aid to the blind program already operates on such a "no-maximum" basis.

I will urge the Legislature when I discuss appropriations in my budget message to examine carefully the prospective needs that may confront the persons depending on old age assistance, aid to dependent children, aid to the blind and the state's public relief assistance during the next two years and appropriate sufficient funds to permit the Director of Social Welfare to raise the standards of assistance for these groups, if needed, to meet further rises in living costs.

* * * * *

By a few simple steps taken at this time, the state can go forward toward the elimination of tuberculosis as a major menace. First, in providing financial aid to local jurisdictions and local sanatorium commissions, it is necessary to recognize the increased cost of the new procedure in treatment of the disease.

In the second place, the state can, by passing enabling legislation, consolidate its treatment facilities into a small number of more adequately equipped sanatoria. Such legislation should also permit local sanatorium commissions, when they deem it advisable, to close their institutions and transfer their remaining patients to other sanatoria. County sanatoria so closed might then be used to considerable advantage for the care of the aged and infirm. For the state to embark on such a program of consolidation at this time will prove to be a good investment, not only from the humane point of view but also financially.

* * * * *

Many county welfare boards have asked that the Legislature make plans for the care of the chronically ill and disabled aged. This matter has been carefully studied by the Legislative Research Committee, and a very fine report has been issued by them covering it. I heartily endorse their report, and I urge that this Legislature consider how more adequate facilities can be provided to meet the needs of several thousand aged persons for whom the proper type of care is not now available.

* * * * *

We are all aware of the difficulties facing the American Indian. A large number of Indians are looking to government for aid because of lack of employment, cultural problems of their own, and uncertain opportunity. The problem is further entangled by federal wardships, restrictions of living on closed reservations or allotted lands, and the general lack of a program designed to bring them into the productive stream of our society. Recently federal resources have been withdrawn, and the plight of many of our Indian people has become acute. I suggest that the Legislative Research Committee or a joint committee of the Legislature be appointed to study this problem. In the meantime, adequate financial aid should be extended to counties with concentrated Indian populations to provide care for Indians in need.

* * * * *

Several years ago the Legislature very wisely created county welfare boards to administer the several welfare programs in each county. Several hundred responsible citizens serve as members of these boards, and they are performing their duties in an energetic and efficient manner—in some instances at considerable personal sacrifice. In twenty-two counties direct relief is still administered by townships. In the interest of better ministration to the needy, more efficient operation, and the elimination of jurisdictional disputes between townships over relief cases, I strongly urge that the Legislature enact a law empowering county welfare boards to administer direct relief in all counties of the state.

* * * * *

In accordance with the recommendation of the State Association of District Judges, I should like to suggest that you provide for a commission to be appointed by the Governor to study the laws of Minnesota relating to divorce, particularly as they relate to children.

* * * * *

There is a new problem of interest since the Legislature last met, that of helping the displaced persons of Europe find a new home and new hope. Minnesota has taken a role of leadership in this effort from the very outset. We have done so because we recognize our obligation, as Christians, to give aid to these suffering men, women, and children without a place of refuge as the result of war. It is essential in our state that there be a plan to take care of our quota of these unfortunate people who settle here. This, in addition to a warm welcome, will make these uprooted wanderers real assets to our communities and not objects of charity.

In order to properly coordinate the efforts of this state in behalf of displaced persons, I recommend legislation empowering the Director of Social Welfare to administer and supervise the program for displaced persons in the state, with a modest appropriation for this activity.

* * * * *

Although the main outlines of our Social Welfare program in Minnesota are well accepted by the people, we must never relax our vigilance in caring for all those in need. This is one of our great human goals.

5. PUBLIC HEALTH

The protection of public health is another important aspect of our first objective. The last Legislature wisely provided aid to counties for the employment of public health nurses. As a result fifteen more counties have provided for nurses and twelve have added nurses to an existing program —and this despite the shortage of qualified nurses.

It has been gratifying to note the growing interest in public health problems. In recent months I have attended seven community health day programs in various sections of the state. At these meetings citizens of several counties have joined together to discuss and to develop plans to improve public health programs. This interest indicates the willingness of the people to pay the small costs necessary for expanded community health services. I appreciate the fact, too, that many members of the Legislature contributed materially to the success of these efforts by participating as speakers and discussion leaders at these meetings. I want to stress the importance of local public health services to enable us to meet the great challenge of present health problems.

6. HUMAN RELATIONS

No problem in modern life is of greater consequence than that involved in our sixth goal—the improvement of our human relations. In no area is there a more astounding difference between our technical knowledge and progress on the one hand, and our unwillingness to make application of that knowledge to harmonious living together, so absolutely essential to the functioning of a democracy.

The wonders of science are all about us, yet the wisdom to utilize these wonders in building the "Golden Age of Man" is sadly lacking. Science has progressed with dazzling rapidity; the development of our human relations has crawled along at a snail's pace. Our solemn duty is to build bridges of understanding across the tragic chasms of racial, religious, and national differences. Unless these social tensions are mitigated—and that right soon—they threaten to wrench the fabric of our society and tear it into shreds.

We are still seeking the simple formulas which can bring world peace at the conference table, agreement in the factory and workshop, and tranquility to the family circle. The ominous shadows of greed and passion hang over a world which lives in dark dread of atomic and bacteriological warfare. There is no pat remedy for our plight. Look for no miracles. Only enlightenment in human relations can bring in the new era of unity and peace. Chemists, biologists, and engineers are required to build the better world. There must be no vacation for them. But the greatest need for our day is for human engineers—human engineers who will take the products of science and use them with compassion and understanding, not to the hurt but the healing of men.

Two great wars have been fought and won in a single generation to preserve the cherished ideal of equal opportunity. This ideal we must now translate into the problems of our daily life.

Every worker in our free society has a right to be judged and selected for a job on the basis of his abilities, demonstrated skills and background of experience. Certainly democracy suffers a tragic defeat every time a member of its society finds the doors of industry closed to him because of the color of his skin, his religious faith, or his particular race.

* * * * *

Our problem is to find the proper way by which we may successfully clear away these restrictive bonds which are crippling the effective operation of our democracy. To encourage the practice of democracy in employment requires an aggressive program of education and legislation.

The Governor's Interracial Commission is admirably performing the educational task. To meet the legislative need, a fair employment practice law should be passed. Such a law will benefit employers rather than harm them, for the reason that the labor market for employers will be increased. Employers will not lose the opportunity of selection. The law is designed to prevent prejudice. Such a law will make it possible for members of minority groups to prepare themselves, in the knowledge that they will receive a fair opportunity in employment.

A fair and carefully prepared bill was introduced at the last session. It will be presented again, and I respectfully urge you—in fact, I plead with you—to give it your support.

Suggestions by the Interracial Commission for the strengthening of our civil rights statute should also receive your support. As you know, I have indicated a desire to integrate Negroes into our National Guard. Federal regulations have prevented this. I believe that the Legislature should memorialize the President to change the regulations so as to make this possible. I further believe that our state constitution should be amended so as to include a specific provision against discrimination in our National Guard.

Here again the people of Minnesota have the opportunity, and the duty, to blaze new paths through a wilderness of ignorance and prejudice to our goal of better human relations.

7. LAW ENFORCEMENT

The people of the state have indicated in no uncertain terms their belief that our laws should be observed and enforced. The continued strengthening and support of our law enforcement program is our eighth human goal.

There still is laxity in enforcement in certain areas of the state, particularly with reference to the sale of liquor to minors. We have received a large number of letters in the Governor's office from heartsick parents, pleading for help in relation to this problem. We have an obligation to protect our youth from the callous consciences of some unscrupulous persons in this business. I therefore recommend uniform closing hours for beer and liquor establishments throughout the state, with a twelve o'clock closing on week days and one o'clock on Saturdays. Because of the conflict of closing hours existing at the present time, we have migrations late at night from one community to another, from the earlier to the later closing establishments, with traffic hazards and all the other serious implications involved.

Secondly, I think the Legislature should provide the power of arrest for the Liquor Control Inspectors, just as the Highway Patrolmen and Game Wardens have the power of arrest in their respective fields. You will recall that when the question was considered at the last session, objection was raised that this was giving the Governor too much authority and that enforcement belongs with the local units of government. I heartily concur in the idea that enforcement responsibility belongs fundamentally in the local communities. But in many of the local communities the laws are *not* being enforced as they ought to be and the people themselves are continually asking the Governor's help in bringing about effective enforcement. I submit that there is a responsibility at the state level to guide, supervise, and lead the way to better enforcement. This is a reasonable request as long as we are called upon to help the local communities.

The fundamental concerns which motivate me in this matter of law enforcement are now, as they always have been, two-fold: first, a deep conviction as to the necessity of protecting our boys and girls; and, second, a profound respect for the sanctity of law as being the very foundation of democratic government.

8. LABOR-MANAGEMENT RELATIONS

The ninth of our human goals lies in the field of labor-management relations. In my first inaugural message I said:

"I do not believe that stability will be achieved

by punitive methods against labor. I do not believe that the great mass of employers want to see restrictive methods used against our workers, nor do I believe that the rank and file of working men and women want to see unfair methods used against employers. Both groups, in the main, prefer to adjust their differences peacefully—through negotiation rather than through conflict—and we should continue to keep the emphasis on conciliation, with a minimum of restriction."

After two years of experience in the settling of labor disputes in the Governor's office I am confirmed in the conviction there stated.

The well-being of our economy is directly dependent upon the ability and willingness of labor and management to work together. The Minnesota Labor Relations Act, which was enacted in 1939, has helped make possible a decade of good labor relations. I believe that the record since its passage indicates its adequacy. It contains a minimum of compulsion and regulation. It wisely places its reliance upon a maximum of voluntary participation of labor and management for its success.

The time has come when we must stress the human element in management-labor relations. Labor cannot advance alone. Management cannot advance alone. We shall not advance at all unless we advance together. It is important, then, that labor shall meet its obligation to perform a full day's work for wages received. And management must fulfill its obligation to treat the laborer as a human being and not as a cog in a machine.

Teamwork must be the basic objective in labor-management relations.

Related to the labor-management problem is the matter of employment and security.

I strongly recommend that the Legislature give favorable consideration to increasing the weekly amount paid as unemployment compensation to jobless workers. Present rates were established in 1943, and the higher living cost now prevailing is ample reason for authorizing an increase.

In addition, the employment security law should be amended to remove inequities in sections denying payment of benefits to persons who, through no fault of their own, are made idle as a direct result of a labor dispute.

* * * * *

A second matter related to the labor-management goal is the matter of workmen's compensation.

There are a number of proposals in connection with it and other problems affecting workers which merit attention. Among the proposals which I feel you should consider are: (1) Establishment of rehabilitation centers where the advantages of modern therapy can be utilized to assist in the rehabilitation of injured workers, (2) provisions for increased benefits in certain types of cases under workmen's compensation, (3) provision for 48-hour work week for women workers, and (4) added protective regulations for minors employed.

The state itself is an employer, though in a special category. It is recommended that you provide a 40-hour week for all of our employees, including the members of the State Highway Patrol. Most of our employees are now working under a 40-hour week and it is only fair that it be made uniform for all employees.

It is further recommended that you give careful consideration to means of liberalizing and strengthening the employees' retirement benefit program.

* * * * *

Through cooperation between the legislative and executive branches of our government, and supported by the great mass of the people of our state, these human goals represent a program, the achievement of which will constitute a worthy monument in this our centennial year.

We recognize the fact that the mere presentation of these goals is not enough. Hard logic and common sense dictate that we undergird our social and humanitarian programs with a solid bedrock of material resources.

Therefore, in support of the human goals for which we strive we proceed to the second major portion of our message, which has to do with providing the economic means by which these goals may be attained.

II. *THE ECONOMIC MEANS OF ATTAINING OUR GOALS*

1. CONSERVATION

The first of these economic means is the conservation of our natural resources. This is one of the gravest problems that confronts the Legislature. All of our aims for better living will fail if we fall short in protecting our heritage of natural resources—from which, directly or indirectly, we draw all income, all tax revenue, and all the means of our existence. We rob the future by wasting today.

Marvelous Minnesota! A land blessed by Providence, a land which has been given fertile soil, vast virgin forests, sparkling waters, immense deposits of iron ore, teeming wild life, scenic beauties, and all the bountiful gifts of nature. From these natural gifts has come the wealth and the progress of our first one hundred years. Have we been faithful stewards of these gifts which God has given? Have we lived on the fat of the land? To put it bluntly: we have made mistakes; there has been selfish and foolish exploitation; there is danger that unless we mend our ways, those who follow in the next century will be left to pick the bones. As we take stock today, we find that large sections of nature's once well-filled storehouse are becoming ominously bare.

Many of our lakes and streams, the pride of Minnesota, are being filled with silt deposits or contaminated by pollution. Depletion of our forests from cutting, fires, and other losses is going on over the years faster than the current growth. Game and fish are hard pressed by a greatly increasing demand for them in the face of steady shrinkage of their habitat. Another record year of production has cut deeper into our diminishing stock of high-grade iron ore. Any way we turn, we face an inevitable shortage of the means of survival at no distant date unless we act vigorously to stop the depletion that is now going on.

* * * * *

No single natural resource is more crucial to the continued prosperity of our state than the fertility of its soil.

I especially call your attention to the importance of appropriating $100,000 to the state soil conservation committee so we may intensify our efforts to carry out good soil management. This program is essential to the conservation not only of the soil, but also of lakes and streams, forest, and wildlife.

Our forests, the chief support of a large section of northern Minnesota and one of the mainstays in our state's economy, also deserve your attention.

The field of water conservation and water pollution control also require action.

Special consideration is due to our valuable iron ore resources, which constitute the chief support of many mining communities, a major factor in the economy of the state, and a prime essential for national defense.

* * * * *

Another problem of conservation is the maintenance of our state park system. Our system of parks compares favorably with any in the country.

Our state parks provide opportunities for all our people to enjoy the out-of-doors. Medical men tell us that outdoor recreation is not a luxury but a necessity for health and welfare. It is a potent antidote for juvenile delinquency and an important factor in our youth conservation program. I therefore recommend increased appropriations to meet this urgent need.

* * * * *

Thus, briefly, we have sketched the first bulwark of our human goals, the conservation of our natural resources. It is for us in the present to redeem the losses of the past and to guarantee the gains of the future. Thus we will prove ourselves good stewards of what God has given us and assure for ourselves and our children the means for a more abundant life.

2. AGRICULTURE

No foundation for the attainment of our human goals is more fundamental than the continued prosperity of agriculture.

Through the investment in research we can provide new opportunities for wise utilization of our farm resources. It will pay us, as it has in the past, to provide our university scientists with funds to carry on projects seeking to improve the quality and the quantity of farm produce.

The 1947 Legislature provided a great new field of research at the Rosemount project. Although this work has been underway only a few months, it has already shown the wisdom of the investment.

I know that you will also want to provide for the continued development of the new school for veterinary medicine, thus meeting a need long felt in this great livestock-producing state.

* * * * *

In closing this message, I want to say that I shall endeavor to work with all of you during this important session in a spirit of understanding and an appreciation of the difficult problems facing us.

We cannot afford to permit political differences to interfere with our common obligation to meet the needs of our people and build a stronger state. There is too much at stake.

I should like to quote the words of a famous statesman:

"I would advise, therefore, that your legislation should be such—as will guard equally, the rights of labor and the rights of property, without running into ultraisms on either hand—as will recognize no social distinctions, except those which merit and knowledge, religion and morals, unavoidably create—as will re-press crime, encourage virtue, give free scope to enterprise and industry—as will promptly, and without delay, administer to and supply all the legitimate wants of the people—laws, in a word, in the formation of which will be kept steadily in view the truth, that this Territory is destined to be a great State, rivalling in population, wealth and energy, her sisters of the Union; and that, consequently, all laws not merely local in their objects, should be framed for the future as well as the present . . ."

Timely though they be, these words are not those of a living statesman. They are the words of Governor Alexander Ramsey as he spoke to the first Minnesota Legislative Assembly in 1849. The setting for the address of the first Governor was quite different from ours today. He spoke in no great edifice of marble; his address was delivered in a temporary capitol in the Central House, a small wooden hotel on the St. Paul river front. The hotel dining room was used for the joint session of the two legislative bodies; a flag was hoisted on the staff in front of the hotel; an Indian sat on a nearby rocky bluff and watched the proceedings.

* * * * *

Though outward circumstances are utterly changed, we need to emulate, as we face our next century, the courage, the vision, and the spirit of sacrifice which animated the founders of our state. The road before us today, as it was one hundred years ago, is rocky and fraught with peril. Too many of us fail to appreciate the hazards and are like the young American who arrived in Zermatt, Switzerland, and seeing the towering peak of the Matterhorn, asked, "What's the name of that big rock?" When told it was one of the most famous of the Alpine summits, he said, "Do you think I could get up there this afternoon?" Little did he know the story of the peak's costly conquest, of the lives it had taken, of the hazards still involved in the ascent. So is liberty, a decent society, a lasting peace, each a majestic mountain peak. How much do we really want them? Do we appreciate their cost? Are we willing to pay the price for them and sacrifice for them?

The pioneers of 100 years ago did not hesitate to pay the price for a strong society. They did not allow their spiritual values to be smothered beneath the false riches of material possessions. May the high idealism, the courage, the selflessness, and the implicit faith in God which characterized the founders of Minnesota inspire us. In the same spirit of consecration may we also move ahead to our next and even greater century of advancement, building together a nobler Minnesota.

CHAPTER XVI

Dawn of a New Day

The world is in turmoil and crisis. The year 1951 and those years immediately ahead may well be the "Hinge of Fate" upon which the destiny of the world turns. We are a part of the life and death struggle of two totally opposed philosophies of life. The antagonists are communism on the one hand, which denies God and places its faith in naked force and materialistic values, and on the other the democratic way of life, which places its faith in the Fatherhood of God and the Brotherhood of Man. Under communism man is a vassal and the State is supreme. Under our philosophy each man is uniquely precious because, like an ancient coin of gold, he is stamped with the image of the King.

It seems but yesterday. It was only four years ago, in this same place, that we acclaimed the end of hostilities of World War II. We met then with a strong hope for the achievement of world peace based on the concepts of the United Nations.

Today, we do best if we resolutely face a supremely unpredictable future. We know not what the morrow may bring. It may be peace. It may be war—war of such proportions and ferocity that all previous struggles will in comparison appear as preliminary skirmishes.

In these circumstances, for us to make plans based on specific prediction of the future is both foolish and impossible, yet hazards and uncertainties must not sap our courage nor paralyze us into inaction. Any plans we make or any programs we establish which are based on eternal principles of justice and humanity will always prove valid and right as the future unfolds.

The price we shall be required to pay for freedom will be great, but the cost of slavery is infinitely greater. The price of freedom includes far more than money, materials, and military might. The intangible demands made upon us are greater than these. Each of us as a citizen is charged with a personal responsibility. Our state government must reflect this sense of personal responsibility. We must discipline ourselves to absolute integrity and dedicate ourselves to the advancement of human values. Honesty and humanity in government must constantly be our goal. In times of complacence and plenty it has too often been assumed that the accumulation of material resources is sufficient for safety and survival, but in times of crisis and disaster our sense of values must change. In such times, our survival will depend not upon material resources, but upon human and spiritual values.

The Legislature has in past sessions demonstrated its faith in these human values by legislation enacted in support of education, mental health, youth conservation, law enforcement, and other progressive measures.

At this session, conditions over which neither you nor I have any control make our task even more difficult. The spiral of inflation and the zooming costs of our military establishment reduce the value of the dollar and limit the sources of revenue for the operations of state government. In spite of these and other difficulties which might be mentioned, our plain duty is to bend ourselves to the task of meeting the challenges of the hour. We pledged the people to continue to work for honesty and humanity in government. We must keep this promise.

When we speak of "humanity" in government, we think of it in its broad sense as including every program by which we meet human needs and by meeting them undergird our human resources.

Similarly, "honesty" in government encompasses not only integrity in financial matters, but also a fair and equitable approach to every practical problem relating to our economic resources.

With the terms thus broadly defined, my message to you will be divided in two main divisions. The first deals with the whole area of our human and social goals. The second is concerned with the prerequisites for the attainment of these goals.

I. HUMANITY IN GOVERNMENT

1. *Home and Family*

Of the new proposals dealing with "humanity in government," the one closest to my heart is the one I shall now discuss, a plan for the strengthening of the home and family life.

The nation which fails to give integrity to the home will ultimately pass into oblivion.

It is in the home that the lessons of mutual responsibility, of self-sacrifice, are learned. The family is the only true democracy, whose motto is "One for all and all for one." The weak and the young as well as the wise and the strong have equal claims upon the family resources. If one member suffers—all suffer with him; if one member rejoices, all rejoice with him.

It was in the patriarchal family, expanded into the clan, that humanity learned the first lessons of government and social unity. The sense of social solidarity developed slowly in society at large, but its roots lie deep in family life.

The Interim Committee for the study of family life has done an excellent job. Its report has already aroused widespread and favorable reaction. All the recommendations in the report deserve your careful consideration.

The report emphasizes the necessity for diagnosis and therapy in dealing with family difficulties and the use of all available facilities to remove the causes of family breakdowns.

The old adage says, "Count to ten before you swing." This homespun piece of advice has prevented many a fist fight. Application of the same principle has been effective in the area of labor relations where the "cooling off" period has prevented strikes and lockouts. We may be certain that a principle which has proved effective in these and other areas will apply with equal strength to conflicts in family life.

Therefore, I favor legislation requiring a period of conciliation before a divorce action may be commenced. I also recommend the committee's proposal that judicial procedures be established to provide specialized treatment to strengthen family ties before they are broken in divorce.

You have dignified these legislative halls in past sessions by enacting farsighted and effective laws for the preservation

of our state's human resources. Here again we have the opportunity to pioneer and, at relatively small cost, to undergird that basic unit of our society, the home.

2. *Mental Health*

In Minnesota, "snake pits" and bedlams have disap-
peared. We are building the House of Hope. Our official
policy as a state is to recognize that mental illness is a sickness and a medical problem to which there should be attached
absolutely no shame or stigma.

Having made a start, the temptation will be strong to
stagnate and stop in our drive for a really adequate mental
health program.

At the last session you began one of the most magnificent
social structures ever put into law by this or any other legislative body in the country. You passed the mental health act
and backed it up with money. By doing this, you gave a new
lease of hope to tens of thousands of people who have loved
ones suffering from a mental sickness.

I can report a substantial improvement in the care and
treatment of the mentally ill. The health of our patients is
better; mechanical restraints have been virtually eliminated;
overcrowding has been relieved; increased personnel has
made possible new programs of recreation and therapy. Our
patients are better clothed, and the single standard of food
makes them the best fed patients of any state hospital system
in the nation. A beginning has been made in research in out-
patient clinics and in other aspects of our mental health work.

We have laid the foundation for the House of Hope. Upon
this foundation we must continue to build. It is not enough
to hold the line. We must press the attack against the citadels

of the asylum past. The measure of our accomplishment must never be a smug complacency as to the rank we hold in comparison with other states. The only valid satisfaction is to be found in fully meeting the needs of these maligned and forgotten people, whose only hope lies in our compassion and action.

The most urgent immediate need is for a new school for mentally deficient children. The overcrowded conditions at our Faribault school are indescribable—they are a disgrace to Minnesota. In spite of unusual ingenuity and several emergency measures, there are 800 families whose children are being denied opportunity for *any* adequate care or treatment whatever. Of these, several hundred are acute emergency cases. Imagine it! I appeal to you as men with a sense of justice and compassion, and I appeal to the people whom you represent. These children and their parents have endured unspeakable physical and mental suffering. We must not keep them waiting any longer.

Another part of the House of Hope which we must continue to build is in the area of medical treatment of alcoholism, improved care of those aged who have nervous disorders, expanded preventive services, and, above and beyond all else, intensified research, beginning at once, into the causes and treatment of mental sickness.

A third section of the House of Hope where humanity demands a change is in the matter of commitment procedure for the mentally ill. The present system causes humiliation to the patient and his family and seems to imply before society that he is a criminal instead of a sick human being. I recommend that the commitment laws be changed to wipe out the shame and stigma here in the same manner as they have been eradicated in our care and treatment of the mentally sick. Finally, you will want to implement with further financial support the constructive program which you inaugurated at the last session.

You have laid the foundation. Into this foundation have been poured the hopes of our patients, the faith of our families, the support of the Legislature, the inspired work of our psychiatric workers on every level, and the concern and compassion of the people of our state.

In mental health, Minnesota has become the symbol of the House of Hope, and the whole nation looks to us for continued leadership. We ought to pray to God that He will keep us in discontent until the day comes when every mentally sick person receives the care to which he is entitled.

3. *Education*

Education is of critical importance in a democracy. Thomas Jefferson spoke for America when he said, "By far the most important bill in our whole code is that for the diffusion of knowledge among the people. No other sure foundation can be devised for the preservation of freedom and happiness."

The American way of life demands that every citizen shall have the right to an education. Its enemies thrive on ignorance and illiteracy. The American ideal of educational equality is far short of attainment. We have a long way to go, and critical times such as these ought to spur us on to a new zeal to provide an education sufficient to meet the demands of the hour. Therefore, I strongly urge you to meet the costs of the educational needs in our state.

In 1947, you made wise revisions in the state aid laws for our schools. Under this program, the biennial appropriations for school aid were substantially increased in 1947 and again in 1949. Costs here as elsewhere have risen sharply. Therefore, I recommend that school aids be increased sufficiently to meet these increased costs.

In our determination to provide good education for every child, we have often sought the counsel of the educational leaders of our state. They have been a real source of strength and support. They recognize as we do that children who are delinquent, mentally retarded, or physically handicapped are equally entitled to educational opportunity; in fact, children in these groups lay claim to an even greater measure of our help.

Therefore, although it is my conviction that the income tax revenues should remain dedicated to common school purposes, I recommend that our definition of such purposes include provision for state aid to the handicapped groups just mentioned. This would give some relief to the general revenue fund, upon which increasingly large and diverse demands are being made and would improve the educational offering for these young people.

Opportunities for in-service training of teachers should be put on a permanent basis, particularly in view of the probable shortage for some years to come.

You should also enact a teachers' salary schedule, guaranteeing that a minimum of sixty-five per cent of school maintenance costs be designated for teachers' salaries. The teachers' retirement law should be changed to permit members to make higher contributions and to have a wider choice of annuity benefits.

These and other steps which we can take will help to attract and retain a high caliber of men and women in the teaching profession.

A possible new use which might be considered desirable for income tax school funds would be that for the assistance of hard-pressed districts in the cost of erection of school buildings. Unusual circumstances, such as a high percentage of publicly owned land, make it impossible for some districts to raise the necessary revenue.

You also have before you the question of extending state aid to junior colleges.

Our state university is celebrating its centennial of distinguished service to Minnesota, our nation, and to the world. It occupies an eminent position among the great universities of our country. The high position it thus holds would have been impossible without the interest and support of the Legislature and the people, and in this historic centennial year you will want to continue your support.

Our five excellent teachers' colleges likewise deserve your continued support in the task of training teachers for our schools.

In Minnesota we have made substantial progress in public education, but Americans must be willing to devote more of their income to education than ever before. Good schools cost money. This is part of the price we are called upon to pay if we are determined to maintain our way of life. Money appropriated for schools is, I submit, an investment from which our state and nation will receive priceless returns.

We in government, as well as professional educators, ought to have a profound sense of stewardship with reference to the money which is appropriated and spent for education. The people have a right to expect that we be continually diligent and alert to improve the substance of what our boys and girls are taught. Accumulation of facts and figures and the sharpening of a shrewd and canny mind for material advantage produce neither happiness for the individual nor benefit to society. Therefore, our educators have an obligation continually to reappraise their courses of study, particularly in the fields of character development, vocational guidance and training, citizenship, and family life.

Humanity in government requires a deep concern for the true happiness of our boys and girls. To this purpose, in the "atomic age," is added the necessity of well-trained and inspired citizenry to assure survival. There are only two choices: To pay the cost or be destroyed, because, as a great historian has stated, "History is a race between education and catastrophe."

4. *Youth Conservation*

"If all the youth of America could speak to us, they would speak with one voice and say, 'We are the future, for in us there lies what through the ages this land shall be. Yet what we are is what you are to us. We are the question to which you make reply.' "

As legislators, you have in the past two sessions made reply to the critical needs of our boys and girls by enacting far-sighted legislation which has already established Minnesota as a leader in the field of youth conservation. And all this at relatively small cost.

What a responsibility! What an opportunity! To salvage and repair youthful lives that have been blighted and damaged, and by positive programs to strengthen and build lives of usefulness and character among children of city and country, of every race, color, and creed, what a privilege!

Two significant state-wide youth conferences have been held, at the last of which more than 2,000 delegates attended representing every section of our state and every walk of life. My recommendations to you are based upon the findings and suggestions of these conferences.

First in importance at this session will be the establishment of a forestry camp, in which young people can be brought into a healthful environment and, under friendly guidance, be taught constructive habits of work and play and be given other training for useful citizenship.

You have previously shown your approval of such a plan, and I am sure you will now be eager to support it with appropriations. Especially will this be true when you consider the fact that the financial cost of this program will be rendered even smaller by useful improvements to our forests and parks.

It is with extreme reluctance that I am not recommending at this session the establishment of a permanent diagnostic center for youthful offenders committed to the Youth Commission. I forego this recommendation because of the great financial demands placed upon our state by the national emergency. The need for such a diagnostic center will remain, and provision for it should not long be delayed.

One of the salutary effects of our youth conservation program is a substantial decline in the number of youthful offenders being kept at Sauk Centre and Red Wing. Their rehabilitation is being accomplished in a home environment. This circumstance has necessitated an expansion of parole and probation services, and you will be asked to provide additional personnel. Such a system has shown itself to be more effective and also far less expensive.

A further increase in Commission personnel will assist in the accomplishment of something even more important. That is the prevention of delinquency. It is cheaper and safer to prevent fires than it is to fight them. The same principle applies with equal cogency to preventing demoralization rather than repairing shattered lives.

Nowhere is humanity in government more dramatically illustrated than it is in our task of salvaging and conserving the lives of our boys and girls. Here again, the cost of a positive program is infinitesimal in comparison with the price which will be exacted if we shirk our duty.

5. *Human Relations*

Right here in Minnesota the problem of human relations must be faced and decided. Therefore, I plead with all my heart and soul for the passage of a Fair Employment Practices Law.

We have made a start. Our Interracial Commission has performed a real service in public education against the ignorance that breeds bigotry. At the last session you wisely appropriated money for the work of this commission.

But this is no more than a start. Surely you will reaffirm your faith in educative force of public opinion by continuing your appropriation for the commission, but the immediate crux of the problem will not be touched until not one of our fellow citizens is deprived of his right to earn a livelihood because of racial or religious discrimination.

By executive order, our National Guard has been opened to Negroes, and I thank God that as our guard units are called up for service they will not be required to be the object of insult and humiliation in addition to making the sacrifices for which they have volunteered.

In the field of civil rights talk is cheap, but our actions shout so loudly that the people of other nations cannot hear what we say.

Right here in Minnesota jobs are still being denied our fellow citizens, not because of incompetence, but because the door of opportunity is slammed in their faces by reason of racial and religious prejudice. To deny a fellow human the right to earn a living for himself and his loved ones for such morally indefensible reasons breaks faith with our American heritage.

The struggle with communism is essentially a spiritual battle. Diplomatic maneuvers and supremacy in arms will never be sufficient to win the hearts of a billion people who, shaking off the shackles of the centuries, are demanding equality as dignified human beings.

The global struggle has its application here in Minnesota.

Your action in passing an F.E.P.C. law will be a devastating blow to the armor of the forces of darkness.

6. *Social Welfare*

The problem of our aged citizens is one of major concern. Much of our past history in meeting our responsibility to elderly people has not been of a hopeful sort, but mainly that of keeping body and soul together. Too often the rewards of survival into old age have been poverty, sickness, humiliation, loneliness, fear, and despair.

This is a problem which grows in magnitude because of the ever-increasing life span of our people. We must overcome the tragic social consequences and the waste of human resources, and we must plan for the continued happiness and usefulness of these people to the extent that it is humanly possible.

Therefore, I recommend that you provide for a Commission on Aging to be appointed by the Governor to study the whole problem of our older folks. Such a commission would give its attention to such matters as the changing structure of our population; the role of government; the human needs of the older citizens and how they can be met; the effects of inflation; family life and housing; and our present and possible insurance and pension requirements.

Two years ago I urged the abolition of a maximum in old-age assistance grants. I again recommend removal of the limit. With the rising cost of living, there is urgent need to at least raise the maximum.

Also the present property limitation for eligibility to old-age assistance was set at $5,000 in 1939. A more nearly comparable figure today would be $7,500, and it is only fair that the limit be raised to that amount.

There remain some twenty counties still using the archaic and wasteful township system of administering relief. Hundreds of examples of hardships are the result. I strongly urge that the county system of relief administration be made mandatory.

To eliminate delay and unnecessary expense in granting aid to needy persons, I strongly urge establishment of a one-year uniform residence requirement in all aid programs.

To help meet an acute shortage of nursing home facilities, I recommend enabling legislation permitting counties to establish convalescent homes for the aged.

To help the permanently disabled, a law should be enacted to permit this state to participate in the new federal aid program which has just been developed.

No category of human need more certainly arouses our sympathy than that of the blind. Several worthy proposals will be presented to you at this session, and I urge their adoption.

The Federal Social Security laws have been amended, and we should adjust state laws to take full advantage of the new procedures. You may also be called upon to decide important issues related to public employees' participation in Federal Old Age and Survivors' Insurance.

Our state laws relating to tuberculosis should be recodified to eliminate obsolete portions and duplications and to make possible more efficient administration.

We can all be proud of our part in the Displaced Persons program, the success of which has earned national recognition. I urge you to extend the authority for this worthwhile activity.

Minnesota took the leadership in the formation of the Governor's Inter-State Council on Indian Affairs, and your interim committee will be reporting to you on this matter. Our goal should be the integration of the Indians into our economy and society. To this end, you should provide for a continuing legislative committee to work with the Federal Government to provide a better living for our Indian citizens.

Our continuing responsibility to provide care for people in need is an important aspect of humane government.

7. *Public Health*

Because of military and civil defense demands on our manpower, with a critical shortage already in sight, the health of every citizen becomes of vital concern in any program for humanity in government.

Two years ago you enacted a constructive public health measure known as the Multiple County Health bill, which holds vast potentialities for the health of our people. A levy of one mill was permitted for such local health departments, but the law has been interpreted to mean that public health nursing services be paid from this same source of revenue. I recommend that the law be amended to permit the entire mill to be used for the local health unit, allowing the locality to provide other revenue for the public health nursing services.

I recommend that authority be given to the Health Department to regulate the fluoridation of water supply.

It is also recommended that the Health Department be given authority to regulate children's camps in the state in the interest of health and safety.

These and other public health measures which will come before you will give an opportunity to enhance the health of our people.

8. *Labor Management Relations*

(a) *Labor Relations Law*

Under our present Labor Relations Law, providing as it does for a minimum of restriction and a maximum of collective bargaining, hundreds of disputes have been settled amicably. Any proposals which might be made to change the law should be carefully scrutinized to see whether they will strengthen or impair the operation of the act.

(b) *Workmen's Compensation Act*

Our Workmen's Compensation Act of 1913 has been a bulwark of security to our workers and their dependents. Over the course of the years many changes in the law have been necessary, and I recommend that a legislative committee review and recodify the law for submission at the next session. I further recommend the liberalization of certain sections of the Workmen's Compensation Act with reference to occupational diseases, back injuries, total disabilities and statutory limitations on temporary total disabilities and permanent partial disabilities. In these and in other respects the law might well be liberalized in order that Minnesota workmen may be compensated fairly for injuries suffered through industrial accidents.

(c) *Women and Children*

Minnesota legislation to protect women and children was passed in 1909. The law as it now stands is inadequate. Recommendations will be made to you by the state Industrial Commission to revise the minimum wage law of 1913 to more adequately protect minors from hazardous occupations and further to limit the hours of work for women and children. I urge that you adopt their recommendations.

(d) *Unemployment Compensation*

Increased living costs make necessary an increase in unemployment benefits. Liberalizing the benefits will not, it appears, make necessary any increase in the unemployment tax rates.

In case of illness or disability, the consequences of unemployment are often more tragic, as the worker has medical expenses and hospital bills in addition to the loss of wages. Nevertheless, under such circumstances, he is not eligible for unemployment benefits. To bridge this gap in the unemployment insurance program, I recommend enactment of a temporary illness and disability law, coordinated with our present unemployment compensation program.

(e) *Voluntary Apprenticeship*

Our Minnesota voluntary apprenticeship program is one of the finest in the nation. One thing we can do to strengthen it in its representation of all sections of the state is to grant reimbursement for attendance at board meetings.

You are urged to act speedily again to extend for two years the law preventing eviction in hardship cases.

You should again consider the means for equitable stand-by rent controls to prevent dislocation and insecurity on the part of both landlord and tenant. The necessity for this law depends on future congressional action.

Legislation may become necessary to facilitate housing because of the expansion of civil defense or military establishments.

In 1947 you anticipated the national expansion of housing legislation and under the laws you enacted, our communities have been among the first in the country to get housing and slum clearance under way.

In order that we may continue to enjoy maximum participation in any national program, we should take such steps as are necessary to meet changing legislation.

I propose that you appropriate a modest sum for research on the problem of costs for home building.

No problem is trivial which affects the American home. Anything we can do at the state level to eliminate slums and secure decent housing for our people is of real consequence.

We have now, with the brevity made necessary in a message of this kind, outlined some of the areas in which you can apply sound principles of humanity to the processes of our government.

There is no hard and sharp line of demarcation between this section and the one that is to follow. The problems of both are intertwined in the lives of our people.

For purposes of clarity and order, I have separated them, and I proceed now to a brief discussion of those matters which may fairly be considered under the broad title of "Honesty in Government."

II. HONESTY IN GOVERNMENT

1. *Law Enforcement*

The menace of organized crime to the life of our nation has been revealed as by flashes of lightning in the reports of investigating groups, most publicized of which have been the findings of the Kefauver Committee of the United States Senate. For my part, I am more determined than ever before that Minnesota shall take the lead in vigilant and vigorous enforcement of the law. I have never been more certain than I am now, that you and I were accurately reflecting the will of the people in ridding our state of the corrupt and degrading slot machine racket.

In order further to protect our people, particularly our youth, I once again urge that the power of arrest be granted to the state Liquor Control Inspectors. The experience of many states indicates the wisdom of such action.

The callous indifference to the welfare of young people demonstrated in some localities by certain saloons, taverns, and roadhouses underlines the necessity of giving authority to our Liquor Control Commissioner to pass upon applications for retail on-sale alcoholic beverage licenses in the same way that he now passes on off-sale liquor licenses.

2. *Efficiency and Economy in Government*

(a) *Governmental Changes*

As state officials, you and I have a double responsibility. On the one hand, it is our duty to consider the needs of our people, and on the other it is our duty to weigh the ability of our people to pay for such programs as will meet those needs. As we gird for national defense, we should be especially careful in balancing our needs against our ability to pay.

One of the places where we must exercise such care is in the organization of our state government.

I am glad to say that from my meetings with governors and officials of other states I believe Minnesota has one of the finest state governments in the country. Eleven years ago, long before the Hoover Commission began to stir interest in reorganizing the Federal Government, Minnesota worked out a simplification and reorganization of its government which put into effect many of the principles now being sought in the national government. We abolished three cumbersome administrative boards and replaced them with single officials to fix responsibility and speed up administrative action. We set up a new financial control plan, under direction of a commissioner of administration, which, as you know, has saved millions of dollars through sound budgeting, careful scrutiny of allotments to state departments, centralized purchasing, and exercise of the power to prevent deficits.

With machinery like this, the people are assured of efficient and economical handling of the state's business. In most of the major state departments, there is direct responsibility to the chief executive. We must not do anything to weaken or destroy this efficient system of government, nor should we make changes solely for the purpose of making change. However, we should continue to seek ways to improve the machinery of government.

The Committee for Efficiency in Government which the Legislature created in 1949 will have numerous recommendations for you to consider. Individuals will differ on the value of these proposals, so you should weigh all of them carefully and approve those which seem to offer reasonable chance for greater efficiency and discard those of doubtful merit.

(b) *Constitutional Revision*

Our 93-year-old state constitution was drafted in the days of the frontier and the oxcart. It is little wonder, therefore, that it does not fit the needs of modern Minnesota with a population of almost 3,000,000 people and a varied economy.

Trying vainly to keep pace with new conditions and demands, we have amended this basic document 75 times. The result has been likened to a patchwork quilt by experts in government. Today, our constitution contains numerous conflicting, obsolete, and unenforceable provisions.

"Honesty in Government" suffers severely by this situation in which we ignore and fail to carry out constitutional provisions. The respect for law is seriously damaged as a result of this laxness.

The 1947 Legislature appointed a special commission to study the needs for constitutional revision, and it unanimously recommended the calling of a constitutional convention.

You can render a lasting contribution to honest, economical and efficient government by setting the wheels in motion for constitutional revision. This can be done by the passage of legislation permitting the people to vote on the question of whether a constitutional convention should be called. Then, the people could vote on the question in the 1952 general election. The call should provide that the people will have an opportunity to vote on the constitution as finally revised.

Interest is growing for the calling of such a convention. Both major political parties have gone on record as favoring it. We should not delay. In 1958 we shall celebrate the centennial of Minnesota statehood. Surely one of the most fitting ways to observe it would be by having the revision completed by that time. There will be no need for hasty action. Sufficient safeguards exist to assure that the people will be given full opportunity for fair representation in a convention and for a chance to pass final judgment at the polls on the product of the convention.

3. *Conservation of Natural Resources*

Honest government cannot shirk its responsibility for conserving those natural resources from which, in the final analysis, we draw all the means of our existence. To be forgetful of this duty would be to break faith with our children and with generations yet unborn.

This is no time to slight conservation work. Instead, we must redouble our conservation efforts to make sure we have the essentials to see us through the arduous trials of national defense and yet preserve a heritage that we can proudly pass on to posterity.

No problem is more critical than the steady depletion and erosion of our topsoil. The State Soil Conservation Committee and the University Agricultural Extension Service will present to you their recommendations for a program to give added impetus to the fight to save our precious soil. I urge its support.

Although progress has been made in water conservation and water pollution control in the past few years, much remains to be done. I recommend that you give your best efforts to the enactment of legislation to strengthen our program of water conservation, drainage, and water pollution control. The Underground Water Resources Committee, which I appointed, has recommended a thorough study of the water problems of the state, and I recommend that you give careful consideration to carrying out the suggestions of this body of experts.

Destructive forces have been eating into our forest resources through the years. We have never provided the means to stop them, although we have done better these past years following World War II. But our program for forest fire prevention and other forest conservation measures is still far short of what is needed.

I further urge your continued support of the expanded game and fish program already inaugurated to the fullest extent that can be financed by revenues dedicated for that purpose.

Our state parks provide means for outdoor recreation for people at low cost, helping relieve the strains of modern living, counteracting juvenile delinquency, and attracting tourists. We have an obligation to maintain these state parks.

In regard to state-owned lands and minerals, I recommend that our present laws relating to state iron ore leases and extensions be studied and revised to insure that the best interests of the state are served; that research on marginal low-grade iron ores and taconite be encouraged and exploration of iron ore and other minerals be promoted; that funds be allotted to examine and classify all state-owned lands that are now unclassified, so as to determine their best use in the public interest; that funds be provided to enable the state to complete necessary surveys and court proceedings so that title may be established to lake bed iron ore.

All possible aid should be given to support conservation education. Nothing is more essential to a successful conservation program than an appreciation of its importance by all citizens.

4. *Agriculture*

Agriculture is the chief industry of Minnesota. Consequently, the welfare of the entire state is dependent upon our best efforts to maintain a healthy and prosperous farm economy.

Furthermore, with the imminent threat of a third world war, Minnesota farmers may be called upon again to meet unprecedented demands for food production. This grim possibility serves to emphasize the importance of providing adequately for agricultural research to aid in the attainment of goals, made more difficult than ever by a growing manpower shortage on farms. It also should bestir us to do a better job of soil conservation.

I can report that programs are underway so that the people of Minnesota may be better served by the State Department of Agriculture, Dairy and Food. One of these projects is an effort to improve the administrative setup for the inspection services of the Department. In cooperation with the United States Department of Agriculture, other projects are being set up to thoroughly study the marketing of Minnesota agricultural products, so as to furnish more information on how to produce better quality products and to more successfully merchandise them. I am sure you will want to provide for the continuation of these studies.

Another important problem is the pressing need for an expanded program to fight brucellosis, commonly called Bang's disease, which seriously threatens our livestock industry and the health of our people. Some months ago, I appointed a committee to make a detailed study of this matter. The committee has done an outstanding service and I know you will want to turn to its report for guidance in developing an effective plan to eradicate this disease in Minnesota.

* * * * *

9. *Other Means to Create Greater "Honesty in Government"*

(a) *Registration of Lobbyists*

I recommend that you enact legislation providing for the registration of lobbyists. In doing so, we would be following the lead of many other states. More and more it becomes apparent that the people ought to have a chance to secure information identifying lobbyists and pressure groups as they seek to influence the state Legislature. It is important that citizens be accorded the privilege of presenting their views to members of the Legislature. I am convinced that only a small minority abuse that privilege. To protect the majority who conduct themselves with propriety, a law calling for the registration of lobbyists would be very helpful. It should be a law provided with adequate means for enforcement.

(b) *Party Designation and Re-apportionment*

In my past two inaugural messages, I have called attention to the values to be derived from adopting party designation for legislative members and the importance of re-apportioning our legislative districts, as specified by the State Constitution. To do these two things is a matter of simple honesty.

* * * * *

In these ten sections I have made brief references to a few problems of vital concern under the general subject of governmental honesty. My message would not be complete if I were to omit mention of two other matters which are of critical importance by reason of portentous world events.

CIVIL DEFENSE

Less than a decade ago we entered World War II. That I must already speak to you about civil defense is utterly disheartening and tragic. But we are again in peril. The President has declared a national emergency, our men are being called to the colors, and our National Guard units have been summoned. Minnesota people, as always, will respond to the emergency.

For the first time in our history, we stand in danger of a sudden devastating attack against our homes. Long range bombers carrying modern weapons of war are capable of striking anywhere with little or no warning. In the event of another war, Mobilization Day and Invasion Day will be one and the same.

The Council of State Governments in October, 1950, drafted a model Act for Civil Defense. The act provides for defense within the state and for compacts between states. Minnesota, like other states, will need legislation covering this subject.

In view of recent federal legislation dealing with air-raid shelters, it will be necessary for you also to consider this phase of civil defense.

WORLD PEACE

As realistic people, we will fully mobilize for civil defense. But it is a dreary business, this digging holes underground in which to provide a precarious and merely physical security. In contrast, there ought to be a new fervency and zeal in our efforts to erect towers of brotherhood and peace.

Surely by now we know the momentous consequences which will follow upon our failure to erect a structure to insure the enforcement of international law.

It is not merely the problem of our own security, though that is a vital part of it. It is not only the Russian or Communist menace, though, that constitutes the present challenge. It is whether our statesmanship can harness the diabolic use of the physical sciences in time to save us from destruction.

The problem will not solve itself; it cannot be shrugged off or left to others. America, because of its pre-eminence in power and in principles, must not be satisfied with a policy of expedience and muddling through.

I respectfully and earnestly urge you to memorialize the Congress to immediately declare that it is a fundamental objective of United States foreign policy to support and strengthen the United Nations and to develop it so that it shall have the power to make, interpret, and enforce world laws adequate to maintain peace and prevent aggression.

We ought to take the initiative in strengthening the United Nations and in securing the allegiance and support of other countries in order that the United Nations will have enough power to prevent war.

On last United Nations Day, October 24, we dedicated the World's Freedom Bell in Berlin, Germany. As I stood there amid the rubble of Berlin in the center of a war-devastated continent, the inscription on the bell came to me with a new note of urgency: "That this world under God shall have a new birth of Freedom." Such a challenge ought to "stab our spirits broad awake" and ought to fire us to new energy and consecration in building the tower of peace.

CONCLUSION

I have appreciated the opportunity to work with you during two previous sessions, and likewise the privilege of speaking to you today about the problems confronting the people of Minnesota.

The times are increasingly ominous. The world is on fire! Hiroshima, Nagasaki, and the burning villages of Korea are but mirrors reflecting the flames of greed and hatred which burn in the hearts of men.

Someone has suggested that the world has come to such a state of hopelessness that a merciful God would do well to change its orbit so as to bring it into fatal collision with a flaming star. But this is the advice of despair. Heroic men will pray that we be given the strength to direct world affairs toward the light of a star of hope, guidance, and courage.

We do confront despair and disillusionment — but we also face challenge and opportunity.

Disappointed in many of our hopes and confused by our failures, we look about us for scapegoats. By faultfinding and accusations, we try to seek to cover up our own past apathy and neglect.

As it has been aptly said, "If, because of blindness or wishful thinking or lack of vision or courage we fail to heed the storm warnings that are flying, a conquering adversary writing the history of a vanished dream of human freedom may say with some justice that we deserved our fate."

In 1863, with the country agonizing in Civil War, Abraham Lincoln made the following statement:

"We have been the recipients of the choicest bounties of heaven. We have been preserved these many years in peace and prosperity. We have grown in numbers, wealth and power as no other nation has ever grown, but we have forgotten God. We have forgotten the gracious hand which preserved us in peace and multitude and enriched and strengthened us, and we have vainly claimed in the deceitfulness of our hearts that all these blessings were produced by some superior wisdom and virtue of our own.

"Intoxicated with unbroken success, we have become too self-sufficient to feel the necessity of religion and preserving grace—too proud to pray to the God that made us. It behooves us then to humble ourselves before the offended power —to confess our national sins—and to pray for clemency and forgiveness."

That is where we need to begin today. By our attitude of self-righteousness and recrimination we accomplish less than nothing. Now if ever is the time for unity. We have all been guilty, and reparation for the past can only be found in building the future. We can build that future in America, and we can build it right here in Minnesota.

Our willingness to pay the price for constructive measures that will strengthen every force for honesty and humanity in our state government will be tangible evidence of our faith in that future.

A wealthy man took a poor boy from the slums of a great city to his lodge high in the mountains. The boy awakened in the morning. The sky was illuminated with the red and gold of the rising sun reflecting on the ice and stone of the rocky pinnacles and blazoned across the sky. The boy rubbed his eyes in wonder and a great fear filled him. Looking at the flaming splendor, he remembered the lurid tenement fires in which people he knew had burned to death. Terrified, he screamed, "Please, sir, wake up! Something awful has happened—the whole world is on fire." His wealthy friend opened his eyes and, seeing the flame pictures of the Great Artist on the tapestried skies, replied, "Don't be afraid, my boy, everything is all right. The world is not burning up. It is just the dawn of a new day."

The world is on fire, but it need not be the holocaust of destruction. It can be and it must be the flaming dawn of a new day.

THE TYRANNY OF WORDS — *Commencement address delivered at the University of Minnesota August 17, 1961*

THE LOSTLINGS OF SOCIETY — *speech before the Annual Meeting of the Georgia Association for Mental Health, Savannah, Georgia, May 19, 1956*

THE HEARTH, THE FLAG AND THE PRAYER — *address at Maryville College, Maryville, Tennessee, November 11, 1960*

ALL GOD'S CHILDREN — *address before a dinner meeting of The Washington Pilgrimage, Washington, D. C., May 2, 1953*

MOLDING MINDS — *broadcast by Station WCFM, Washington, D. C., October 22, 1953 during American Education Week*

BUILDING BRIDGES — *talk on Youth Conservation at State Youth Conference, Columbia, Missouri, April 29, 1955*

THERE IS A DESTINY THAT MAKES US BROTHERS — *speech before the Tenth Anniversary Convention National Association for Retarded Children, Minneapolis, Minnesota, October 8, 1960*

MAKING YOUR LIFE COUNT — *Commencement address, Milton Hershey School — Fiftieth Anniversary Commencement—Hershey, Pennsylvania, June 6, 1960*

POLITICAL PENICILLIN — *address before Zonta International, Chicago, Illinois, June 21, 1951*

THE GREATEST OF THESE IS CHARITY — *address before the National Conference of Catholic Charities, Atlantic City, New Jersey, November 21, 1949*

CHOSEN PEOPLE OF GOD — *address before the General Assembly of the National Council of Churches, San Francisco, California, December 8, 1960*

RULE OF LAW — *speech before the Men's Brotherhood of Mt. Olivet Lutheran Church, Minneapolis, Minnesota, November 7, 1958*

OUR LIBERTY AND A FEARLESS JUDICIARY — *speech before the Annual Meeting of the Massachusetts Bar Association, Plymouth, Massachusetts, June 15, 1956*

WE'VE GOT TO GO OUT—WE DON'T HAVE TO COME BACK — *excerpts from Inaugural Address to the Legislature of Minnesota, St. Paul, Minnesota, January 8, 1947*

MY GREATEST PAINTING — THE NEXT ONE — *excerpts from Centennial Inaugural Address to the Legislature of Minnesota, St. Paul, Minnesota, January 6, 1949*

DAWN OF A NEW DAY — *excerpts from Inaugural Address to the Legislature of Minnesota, St. Paul, Minnesota, January 3, 1951*